The Arrival Kit

A Guide for Your Journey in the Kingdom of God

RALPH W. NEIGHBOUR, JR.

TOUCH PUBLICATIONS
Houston, Texas, U.S.A

For my three sons
Ralph III, Rodney,
and Randall
on the journey
in the Lord.

The Arrival Kit

Published by TOUCH® Publications, Inc.
P.O. Box 7478
Houston, Texas, 77270 U.S.A.
800-735-5865 • www.touchusa.org

International Standard Book Number: 978-1-880828-33-5

TOUCH® Publications is the book-publishing division of TOUCH® Outreach Ministries, headquartered in Houston, Texas.

Find us on the internet: http://www.touchusa.org

TABLE OF CONTENTS

We suggest you use the New International Version
of the Bible when using this book.

WELCOME TO THE KINGDOM

Hi! I'm Ralph Neighbour. In reading Paul's letters, I realized he wrote about his personal experiences. So I have decided to write this material in the style of Paul, speaking directly to you and sharing my own life. The Christ Who dwells in me greets the Christ Who dwells in you — and makes us one! Let's become close friends as we spend these weeks together.

For the next eleven weeks, I'll be your equipper as you learn about our life in Christ. Here are suggestions to make our times together profitable:

- **Read pages 5 through 9 right away. They're very important.**

- **Then, meet me every day, 5 days every week, at a specific time and place.**

- **Give yourself 15 minutes for our times together, more if you desire.**

- **Keep your Bible handy. We'll be looking up lots of scripture!**

- **You'll need a pen. Faithfully complete the activities marked with a:** ✎

- **Remove the Bible memory verses from the centerfold.**

- **Memorize two verses a week, reviewing those already learned.**

I do hope you have a person in your life who is discipling you. Your mentor should use the suggestions in the back of this book for your weekly equipping times.

IS THIS ALL THERE IS TO LIFE?

Did you decide to follow Christ because you saw you were not making the most of your life? Were you searching for a better way? Perhaps you were extremely successful. You had no serious problems to solve. Life was good. Yet, something was missing. Perhaps you were tired of feeling empty inside.

Before you became a Christian did you ask yourself, *"Is this all there is to life?"*

You have now received a priceless gift — *a new, eternal life!* Before you accepted Christ, how many things did you do without God's guidance? Right now it may be impossible for you to imagine what your new life will be like.

I know a man who bought an expensive computer and never bothered to read the manual that came with it. It could do many amazing things, but he remained ignorant of its potential. After tinkering with it for a while, he set it aside. If he had read the instructions, he would have been amazed by its potential. How sad! Don't do that with your new life in Christ. The Bible is your instruction book. We'll learn how to use it as we journey together.

GET THE MOST OUT OF YOUR LIFE

Are you ready to find freedom from anxiety, jealousy, fear, irritation, boredom, resentment, suffering, and *unhappiness*? Are you thinking, *"That's impossible!"* No! It is possible. Your new life in Christ makes it possible. It's one of the special privileges of being a Christian.

Many Christians (and probably many you know) are not experiencing the truths found in this guide. Christ's power should not be evaluated by observing them. Instead, consider the potential that is yours as a child of God.

HAVE YOU DISCOVERED TRUE HAPPINESS IN THE PAST?

I know you've tried hard! But it didn't last, did it? I know you're a sincere person (I hope you know that, too.) So, what's wrong?

Until now, have you believed happiness comes from outside yourself? Have you ever thought like this? *"I'd be happy if . . .*

- *I felt better physically . . ."*
- *I had more money . . ."*
- *I had a better career . . ."*
- *I had better grades at school . . ."*
- *I had different parents, or a different marriage partner . . ."*
- *(or is it something different for your life?)*

In the box below, write what you have thought might bring you true happiness and peace:

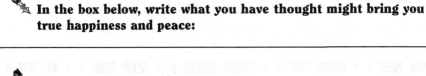

THE CAUSE OF ALL UNHAPPINESS

Are you ready to hear the solution?

It will sound so simple you may dismiss it without understanding how it applies to the very special conditions of your life. There is one basic cause behind all your unhappiness.

Your *expectations* create your unhappiness!

For example, you had an appointment and the person didn't show up. *You were angry!* Your friend made a promise to you and then broke it. *You were frustrated!*

Fear, jealousy, anxiety, irritation, resentment, sadness, disgust, hate — all these emotions are the result of feeling that something must be a certain way before you can feel happy.

Why do you let your happiness depend on people and events? The outside world of life events will *always* make you unhappy. You'll find peace for fleeting moments of time only!

WE HAVE BEEN WRONGLY PROGRAMMED

Computers are designed to do many things. They can become geniuses doing mathematics, or they can used as a tool for web surfing and email. But what they actually do requires a *program* to tell them how to function.

Are you aware of the *"programs"* — mental habits and values — that you've put into your life since your birth? You collected most of them without realizing you were doing so!

For example, we were tiny babies when we first discovered that if we screamed loud enough someone would pay attention to us. As children, we observed the way our parents treated each other and we said, *"I want to act like that,"* or *"I'm never going to act like that!"* Most of our values were picked up like chicken pox: you may not know where they came from, but you certainly know it when you have them!

Think! Where did you pick up the following values?

VALUE:	SOURCE: PERSON, OR ?
Working hard	
Brushing your teeth	
Standing up for your beliefs	
Handling your anger	
Willingness to forgive others	
Mature love (sexual intimacy)	
Meaning of life	
Self-control	

WHAT VALUES HAVE YOU ACCEPTED TO BE TRUE?

. . . That you could have a happy life if you had more money, or more power, or more free time, or more sex, or more "stuff"? How much "stuff" have you accumulated already? *(And how much of it has already been thrown away?)*

After you worked so *hard* to acquire "something" to make you happy, did you immediately worry about losing or damaging it? How did you feel when a *newer model* came out? *Arrgh!*

WHAT STEPS HAVE YOU MADE?

You came to Jesus Christ and asked Him to give you a new life — right? You want to be in love with living.

You have taken the first step. You have not "turned over a new leaf"; instead, *you have turned over your life.* That *is* new!

> *A man received a valuable diamond from his uncle. He worried day and night that someone might steal the diamond. Soon he had dark rings under his eyes! His friend said, "What's the matter with you?" "Oh," he said, "I have this million dollar diamond. I am living in fear that someone will steal it from me." The friend said, "I can help you! Let's go to your bank." They rented a safety deposit box. Protected by steel walls, the diamond was fully protected. The man went home and slept like a baby.*

That's what has happened to you. You have entrusted the priceless treasure of your life to the care of God's Son. Now, for the first time, you can *rest!* You can trust Him with all you are.

WELCOME TO YOUR LIFE IN THE KINGDOM!

When you enter a foreign nation, your first task is to present your passport and get a visa. If your credentials are in order, you are permitted entry.

When you came to the Cross and asked Jesus to cleanse you with His blood, you entered His Kingdom. Paul wrote in Ephesians 2:12 that before you took this step *"you were separate from Christ, . . . without hope and without God in the world."*

In Philippians 3:20, we read that *"our citizenship is in heaven."* You are now a citizen in God's Kingdom! Have you renounced your citizenship in the "kingdoms of this world"?

Jesus spoke about the Kingdom of God 108 times. It was His passion. It's important for you to learn all about the Kingdom of God, because you'll spend the rest of your life — and all eternity — within it. Here are some important facts for you to remember:

THE WORD "KINGDOM" MEANS "REIGN"

Each time you learn about the *Kingdom* of God, substitute the word *reign* for it. A king owns everything in his kingdom completely — the people, the lands, and all the treasures. A king shares his possessions with *no one*. He *reigns* supreme.

Our Lord is not only our Savior, but also our Sovereign, reigning over us as the King of kings! In Luke 1:31-33, the angel said to Mary, *"You will be with child and give birth to a son, and you are to give him the name Jesus. He will be great and will be called the Son of the Most High. The Lord God will give him the throne of his father David, and he will reign over the house of Jacob forever; his kingdom will never end."* King Jesus reigns today!

TODAY, CHRIST'S KINGDOM EXISTS WHEREVER HE REIGNS

In Luke 17:21, Jesus explained that those who searched for His Kingdom in a *location* would never find it. He said, *"the kingdom of God is within you."* When Christ comes to live in our lives, He *reigns* within us. Thus, the Kingdom is made up of all who have declared Him as Lord over their lives. Revelation 1:6 tells us Christ *"has made us to be a kingdom and priests to serve his God and Father."* Therefore, not only are you *in* the Kingdom of God, but *also the Kingdom is in you, because Christ the King is in you!*

IN THE FUTURE, GOD'S REIGN WILL BE GEOGRAPHICAL

God will rebuild this planet as His glorious Kingdom. Peter wrote, *"The heavens will disappear with a roar; the elements will be destroyed by fire, and the earth and everything in it will be laid bare . . . . That day will bring about the destruction of the heavens by fire, and the elements will melt in the heat"* (2 Peter 3:10, 12). In Isaiah 65:17 God said, *"Behold, I will create new heavens and a new earth."* Since our King will return to reign over His Kingdom on earth soon, we should not waste our lives on things that will pass away. In the next eleven weeks, you will learn how to enjoy your new life in God's Kingdom.

YOU WERE FIRST BORN TO FUNCTION IN THIS WORLD

When you were born, you were created with all the senses required to interact with the world around you. First of all, you were able to hear sounds and to taste and smell. You recognized the voice of your mother. Next, you were able to see light. Gradually, you focused your eyes. A while later, you developed the ability to hold objects in your hands. Then, you began to crawl and walk. Later, you began to mimic the language spoken by your parents.

Coordination of your physical senses made it possible for you to use your body in special ways and to reason with your mind. You passed from life as a little child to a young man or woman, finally becoming an adult. At an appropriate age, your reproductive system developed, making it possible for you to create others who are like yourself.

Along with all this, you became a responsible person. You were entrusted with tasks fitting your skills and abilities. You discovered you are a special person. You also may have decided that your *significance* is based on your *performance*. If so, you are a victim in one of Satan's strongest prison cells!

Living in Satan's kingdom has exposed you to evil. Perhaps you have collected a lot of scars from betrayal or rejection or suffered the stabbing pain caused by death. You may have learned to mistrust others and grown to expect to be disappointed by friends. You may have decided that in this world the ones who survive are those who protect themselves. Or, like the rest of us, you may have indulged yourself with luxuries, sex, or even substance abuse.

YOU ARE BORN AGAIN TO LIVE IN CHRIST'S KINGDOM!

When you came to the Cross to transfer the ownership of your life to Jesus Christ, you lacked the spiritual relationship needed to live in the Kingdom of God! Think about this Scripture: *"remember that at that time you were separate from Christ, excluded from citizenship in Israel and foreigners to the covenants of the promise, without hope and without God in the world"* (Ephesians 2:12).

Jesus told Nicodemus in John 3:3, *"I tell you the truth, no one can see the kingdom of God unless he is born again."* In Matthew 13:15 He said, *"For this people's heart has become callused; they hardly hear with their ears, and they have closed their eyes."*

When you were born the second time, it was a spiritual birth. God gave you a whole new set of spiritual senses, making life in the Kingdom possible. *For the first time in your life*, you can hear the voice of the Son of God. Now you can see eternal things. Now you can *walk* in the Spirit.

You must discover how Satan attacks in order to neutralize your Kingdom life. You must discover the way Christ empowers you to build up fellow citizens of His Kingdom. As you begin to grow, you will become a "spiritual father," introducing your friends and loved ones to your King. You will experience the joy of welcoming them into the supernatural world where Christ reigns as Lord of lords.

Are you ready? Let's begin our journey!

Week 1, Day 1
This Unit: Kingdom Lifestyles
This Week: Your New Family
Today: All Babies Have Relatives

Read Ephesians 2:19-22

God arranged His plan so no baby is ever born without a family. Every baby has a mother, a father, and a string of relatives. What would happen if babies were born *without* a mother and father to feed and to care for them? From the moment of birth, babies *should* be surrounded by parents who give tender loving care.

When you became a Christian you entered a new family — a spiritual one. In 1 Timothy 3:15 Paul said, *"know how people ought to conduct themselves in God's household, which is the church of the living God, the pillar and foundation of the truth."* I believe the first Christians immediately organized themselves into "households," cells of 10-15 persons. They didn't use special buildings for their meetings. Instead, they went from house to house, sharing their food and encouraging one another. They were sensitive to each other's needs.

Over the centuries, the people of God moved away from being a *family* to being an institutional *organization*. It took several centuries, but gradually the family life of God's people was replaced by a lot of meetings held in formal buildings called *"churches."*

Actually, the word "church" should never be used to refer to a building. The word "church" comes from a Greek word which means *"called out people."* God's plan was to build a kingdom recognized by *special relationships*.

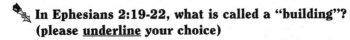 **In Ephesians 2:19-22, what is called a "building"?
(please <u>underline</u> your choice)**

- **A structure erected on a piece of land.**
- **A people who become Christ's dwelling place.**
- **The scripture is unclear; could be either one.**

In our generation, Christians are restructuring themselves to be more biblical. Small groups, or "cells," are forming all over the earth. All life-forms begin with *cells*. This is also true of the church. You will attend "Celebrations" where many cells cluster for praise, worship, and Bible teaching, but your life will be focused on the family unit, your cell group.

Typically, one person will serve the group as the leader and facilitator. Some day, when you have matured, you may also shepherd others as a cell leader. You will soon discover that each member is on a spiritual journey with you. Some will be strong Christians. Others will be weak ones. *(Some will have problems that would make a stone statue weep!)* Observe them as either *models* of the way Christians grow in the faith, or the way Christians allow obstacles to stunt growth.

You, too, will grow along with them. As a little child learns by watching parents and brothers and sisters, so you will begin to develop your own Christian lifestyle by observing how others serve the Lord and struggle with their personal needs.

The most mature believers in the family circle are called "apostles" and "prophets." In Ephesians 2:20, note they are not the *roof* over God's people, lording it over them, but rather they are a *foundation* to support God's people. Of course, the all-important *cornerstone* is Christ Jesus Himself!

**Carefully read Ephesians 2:19-22 again. Answer the questions
below and them with your mentor:**

**1. What does the term "fellow citizens with God's people" mean
to you?**

_____

_____

**2. How does the term "members of God's household" in verse 19
parallel "whole building" in verse 21?**

_____

_____

3. According to verse 22, where does God dwell?

_____

_____

Week 1, Day 2
This Unit: Kingdom Lifestyles
This Week: Your New Family
Today: Growing Up Takes Time

Read Hebrews 5:11-14

Have you just become a Christian? If so, let's compare your *physical* life with your *spiritual* life. While you may be quite mature physically, you are still a spiritual baby. Your Kingdom senses have not yet developed.

Physically, it takes about 20 years to become an adult from infancy. Growing up spiritually also takes time. However, unlike *physical* growth, *spiritual* growth doesn't happen to everyone at the same rate. Furthermore, in the Kingdom you will observe some who have matured in a lopsided fashion — such as studying the Bible but never sharing their faith.

When I was a boy, my daddy took me to a meeting where he was preaching. I shall never forget one person who attended his meetings. Although only as large as a three-year-old, this "child" had a heavy beard on his face! He was actually *32 years old,* but his body and mind had stopped developing when he was only three years old! This can also happen to Christians. They can also fail to properly mature.

In the Hebrews passage for today, the writer was frustrated with his readers. In 5:11-12, what was their problem?

They were S_____ to L_____.

They needed M_____, not S_____ F_____.

You can't tell how mature a Christian is by his or her physical age. Some who have been Christians for years may not have grown as rapidly as others who have belonged to the Lord for months!

FIRST, YOU MUST DIGEST A SPECIAL MILK FORMULA!

Babies develop by drinking milk and progressing to solid food. The writer of Hebrews says it's possible for you to quit growing if you don't progress to solid food! In verses 13 and 14, we are given the exact formula of the food that feeds us, and makes us grow. He says that we must start to drink in the *"teaching about righteousness."* If we do so, we will train ourselves *"to distinguish good from evil."*

God created Adam and Eve *"in his own image"* (Genesis 1:27). During that time, they didn't have to understand the differences of good and evil. Adam and Eve were in the Kingdom, and God was protecting them from the very presence of evil. In fact, God specifically said, *"you must not eat from the tree of the knowledge of good and evil, for when you eat of it you will surely die"* (Genesis 2:17).

Then Satan came to them. Note the words he used to destroy them found in Genesis 3:5: *"For God knows that when you eat of it your eyes will be opened, and you will be like God, knowing good and evil."* That, of course, was a hellish lie! (Satan is the father of lies. You can never trust him to tell the truth!)

Adam and Eve gained not only the *knowledge* of good and evil, they also learned the *consequences* of evil. Paul says, *"their foolish hearts were darkened."* When we are born into a kingdom of this world, we have a moral law within us which enables us to distinguish between good and evil, but, in our fallen condition, we often willfully choose to suppress that knowledge.

DISTINGUISHING GOOD FROM EVIL

All your life, you have lived suppressing this ability! Have you ever watched a one-year-old child grab a pair of scissors when his mother was not watching? Why did she panic when she saw what was happening? It was because that youngster could not distinguish the *good* use of the scissors from their *evil* use. If they were thrust into an eye socket, permanent tragedy would result!

In these first moments of your Kingdom life, it's necessary for you to learn to *distinguish* good from evil. This is the first time in your life you have had the spiritual ability to do that, but it doesn't happen automatically. You must be nourished by the "milk" that teaches about righteousness. 1 Peter 2:2 says, *"Like newborn babies, crave pure spiritual milk, so that by it you may grow up in your salvation, . . ."* The "milk" here is a reference to the Bible.

One person commented, "There's nothing wrong in having sex with a person you're not married to. In fact, I don't even *know* anyone who would argue about that point." In the kingdoms of this world, that might be true. It happens all the time. Getting personal "needs" satisfied seems to be a *good* thing to do, but the results of using another person for self-satisfaction is *evil*, for it doesn't show any respect for the other person.

Babies don't drink milk on their own. It takes many weeks before an infant can even hold a bottle. Others must be responsible for the feeding. That's why your involvement in your cell group is critical to your Kingdom life. You must rely on those who are more mature to feed you.

Week 1, Day 3
This Unit: Kingdom Lifestyles
This Week: Your New Family
Today: Who Are the Fathers?

Read 1 John 2:12-14

> 🌿 **According to this passage, what are the three stages of maturity among those who live in the kingdom?**
>
> **Beginning Stage: C**_____
>
> **Next Stage: Y**_____ **M**_____
>
> **Final Stage: F**_____

During the final three days of this week, we're going to think about the members of your cell group. Spiritually, some have developed more than others. By observing the lifestyles and values of each person, you will gain insights into how much of Christ's presence has been infused into each life.

Did you fill in the words from 1 John 2:12-14? The beginning stage is that of a *child*. In the next stage are the *young men*. In the final stage, we find the *fathers*. We're going to consider fathers first of all, because these are the best models for you to observe. (*"Fathers" describes both men and women.*)

FATHERS HAVE UNIQUE CHARACTERISTICS

> 🌿 **What characterizes a "father" in v. 13?**
>
> "... you have k_____ him who is from the beginning."

> 🌿 **What does verse 13 then say about the "children"?**
>
> "... you have k_____ the father."

Here is an interesting truth. Both "children" and "fathers" *know* the heavenly Father. There are some things about Him that are known by both, because we cannot enter the Kingdom without knowing the King! But there are differences in the way we *know* someone. For example, if you asked me, "Ralph, do you *know* the head of the United Nations?" I would answer, "Yes. I watch television news regularly. I *know* this person."

Then you ask me, "Ralph, do you *know* Ruth Neighbour?" I would answer, "Yes. I *know* her. She has been my beloved wife for many years!"

Do you see the difference? The longer the time you spend with someone, the better you know him or her. In Psalm 25:4, the writer said, *"Show me your ways, O Lord, teach me your paths; ..."* Fathers are those who say, "I have been with our Lord long enough to know His ways. He has moved through my life to minister to

14

others. I know what it's like to sense His presence, and to bow before Him in adoration. *I know His ways."*

THE MOST IMPORTANT THING OF ALL ABOUT FATHERS

According to one dictionary, a father is defined as *"a man who reproduces."* As you get to know those within your cell group and others you meet in your church body, observe those who are bringing the lost to Christ. They are the true fathers in the Kingdom of God! You may discover someone who knows a lot about the Bible, or one who prays a lot, and you may think, "That person is a 'father.'" Perhaps — but the final test of who qualifies to be a father is *one who reproduces*!

Who brought you to know Christ as your Lord? (Write his/her name below.)

_____

There! That's one "father" you already know. How many more can you name?

_____   _____

_____   _____

_____   _____

In John 1:41, we are introduced to Andrew, one of the twelve disciples. We are told that after meeting Jesus *the first thing he did was to find his brother Simon and tell him, "We have found the Messiah."* Andrew was a father to his own brother!

Spiritual fathers don't stop at introducing people to Christ. True reproduction happens when fathers pass down their knowledge of *the Father* to the children. Spiritual fathers don't leave baby Christians as orphans. Instead, they give their lives away, putting others and their needs before themselves. Go out of your way to spend time with such persons. The Spirit of Christ is moving within them. They are being used to draw others into the Kingdom. If it were not for one or more "fathers" who knew Christ and who took time to know you also, you would still be drifting in the darkness of Satan's kingdom, wouldn't you?

Week 1, Day 4
This Unit: Kingdom Lifestyles
This Week: Your New Family
Today: Who Are the "Young Men"?

Read 1 John 2:13-14; Ephesians 6:11-17

**In 1 John 2:13-14, what are the qualities of the "young men?"
(Check all correct answers below:)**

☐ They have overcome the evil one.

☐ They are strong.

☐ The word of God lives in them.

☐ None of the above is correct.

☐ All of the above are correct.

The best athletes seem to be those in their late teens and early twenties. They have lived long enough to develop coordination and muscle skills and to gain experience in playing sports. In the same way, a spiritual "young man" has grown past the child stage of the Christian life and has some "battle scars" from bouts with Satan. Someone has said, "You can't fight the battles *without* until you have learned how to fight the battles *within!*" You may refer to the inner battles as "weaknesses" in your life, but try to think of them like "strongholds."

A *stronghold* is a fortified place where a power has control. However, the power doesn't have *total* control of everything — it has control only where the *stronghold* exists. The word is used 18 times in the Bible to refer to battle conditions where armies hid in "strongholds." It is also used to describe a Christian with an inner condition where Satan still has power to control.

Paul taught about strongholds in 2 Corinthians 10:4: *"The weapons we fight with are not the weapons of the world. On the contrary, they have divine power to demolish strongholds."* In the next verse, he describes what he means by "strongholds": *"We demolish [reasonings] and every [high thing] that sets itself up against the knowledge of God, and we take captive every thought to make it obedient to Christ."* The words in brackets are the literal Greek meanings and help us to see that strongholds all involve our thoughts. The term "high thing" is a reference to those in Genesis 11:4 who started to build *"a tower that reaches to the heavens, so that we may make a name for ourselves and not be scattered over the face of the whole earth."* Satan's desire is to encourage the Christian to question God and to glorify the self instead of the Lord Jesus. He will fill our minds with fear, skepticism, and doubt if we permit him to do so.

Check the fears you have :

- ☐ **Something bad may happen to my loved ones.**
- ☐ **My job is in danger; I may face a financial crisis.**
- ☐ **Will I be able to meet my obligations?**
- ☐ **I may die from a terrible disease.**
- ☐ **My life has no value in the eyes of others.**

Did the list include YOUR fear? if not, write it below:

_____

Strongholds often include lust, pride, bitterness, unforgiveness, grudges, jealousy, covetousness, envy, and other similar feelings. Before you entered the Kingdom, these may have been a constant part of your thought life. Christ wants to set you free from them. You don't have to be crippled by these strongholds any more!

In Ephesians 6:11-17, there are six implements which the "young man" puts on as he faces Satan. List them below:

_____   _____

_____   _____

_____   _____

Note: this armor is defensive in nature. There's nothing to protect the back of the soldier. Why?

- ☐ **Satan never attacks from behind.**
- ☐ **We are never to turn our backs to Satan.**
- ☐ **Christ has already won our battles.**
- ☐ **All three of the above are correct.**
- ☐ **One of the top three is not correct.**

Week 1, Day 5
This Unit: Kingdom Lifestyles
This Week: Your New Family
Today: Who Are the "Dear Children"?

Read Galatians 4:19; Ephesians 4:15; 1 Thessalonians 2:7-8

Children are special people. They are totally trusting and transparent. At the same time, they lack good judgment because they are inexperienced. They may step into dangerous situations without knowing the consequences of their actions. Until they understand their world, they need continual help.

In Galatians 4:19, Paul writes to Christians who are "dear children." He likens himself to a woman agonizing in childbirth. His birth pains are caused by his desire for Christ to be "formed" in them. Yet, in Galatians 2:20 Paul already said, *"Christ lives in me."* In what way did he mean that Christ needed to be "formed" in them?

He knew that the full character of Jesus Christ had not yet developed in their lifestyles. In Ephesians 4:15, he shared how that maturing takes place: *"speaking the truth in love, we will in all things grow up into him who is the Head, that is, Christ."*

The study of the Scriptures is a very important ingredient in the growth of "dear children," but it must include relationships with fellow believers who can "speak the truth in love." There are many things in the lives of "little children" they cannot comprehend without the help of others who love them. In your new family — your cell group — others will see needs in your life, revealed to them by the Lord, which will help you grow. The Bible says we are to "build up" *(edify)* one another. As a new Christian, you may expect the "young men" and "fathers" in your cell to care for your special needs.

Paul wrote in 1 Thessalonians 2:7, *"but we were gentle among you, like a mother caring for her little children."* Your cell group is your Kingdom family. Their task is to help Christ be formed in you. In 1 Thessalonians 2:8, Paul expressed the spirit of true believers in cell groups when he wrote, *"We loved you so much that we were delighted to share with you not only the gospel of God but our lives as well, because you had become so dear to us."*

18

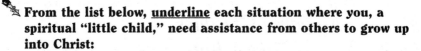 **From the list below, <u>underline</u> each situation where you, a spiritual "little child," need assistance from others to grow up into Christ:**

- **Protection from false teachings and cults**
- **Assurance that you are truly a child of God**
- **Ways to get rid of "old baggage" left in your life**
- **Encouragement when struggling with a problem**
- **The meaning of baptism and the Lord's supper**
- **Counsel from fathers who know the Scriptures**
- **Prayer for healing of your body when sick**
- **Comfort in times of distress or calamity**
- **Others (specify):** _____

_____

Paul often refers to specific needs in the lives of new believers. For example, he shows concern about their being taught that they had to keep a bunch of rules to be a Christian. He made strong statements against that teaching. He also taught new believers not to abuse spiritual gifts by using them for personal pleasure. He was distressed when some immature Christians joined cliques, groups separating themselves from the rest of the Body of Christ. He constantly "mothered" new Christians!

By reading Paul's letters to the churches (i.e. Galatians, Romans, Titus) you begin to discover his concerns. Paul's writings are loaded with comments that will apply to your new life in Christ. You will be amazed at how pointed some of his statements are about the life you now live.

Have you ever seen a child enjoying some ice cream, and an adult asks, "Will you give me some, too?" If the child frowns and refuses to share, it reveals a selfish streak. But if the child joyfully offers a spoonful of ice cream, great joy comes to both the one giving and the one receiving!

Share the insights you have received from reading your Bible in your cell group meetings. In so doing, you will be taking one of your first "baby steps" toward learning how to bless others. Remember — whenever the Lord speaks to you, whatever He gives _you_ will bless _others_.

Don't sit back waiting for the more "knowledgeable" cell members to say everything. You might think that you don't know the "right" answer. Your cell group is not a classroom. We are _all_ to be "edifiers" in the family. In other words, you must let God move through you so that other cell members are encouraged by what you do and say. Share what God has put on your heart. Don't just take and take.

From the very start of your Christian life, learn to give out what the Lord gives to you! Sharing your experiences with Him, along with Scripture, is a "baby step" in learning to build up others. _Try it! Others will like it!_

Week 2, Day 1
This Unit: Kingdom Lifestyles
This Week: Let's Take a Tour
Today: Heaven and Earth

Read Luke 17:20-21

Our Lord taught us to pray to the Heavenly Father in this manner: "Your kingdom come, your will be done on earth as it is in heaven" (Matthew 6:10). When we pray we are asking God to reign on the earth just as He reigns in heaven. God's kingdom activity links "the earthly realm" with "the heavenly realm."

HOW DOES THIS KINGDOM STUFF WORK?

You and I live in God's created world, earth. The earth is made up of that which we can feel, see, hear, taste, and smell. Before you entered into the Kingdom of God, the stuff that happens on the earth was all that you knew.

Now you know that there is more to life than what happens on the earth. You know that God lives in heaven. *"Look down from heaven and see from your lofty throne, holy and glorious"* (Isaiah 63:15). It is also the place where the Father has raised Christ from the dead and *"seated him at his right hand in the heavenly realms"* (Ephesians 1:20). When we became citizens of the Kingdom, Ephesians 2:6 says that *"God raised us up with Christ and seated us with him in the heavenly realms in Christ Jesus."*

There is a third reality that you may never have heard of. I call this place the *"battleground."* This is the unseen arena where Satan enters into battle. Ephesians 2:1-2 tells us: *"As for you, you were dead in your transgressions and sins, in which you used to live when you followed the ways of this world and of the ruler of the kingdom of the air, the spirit who is now at work in those who are disobedient."* Ephesians 6:12 teaches, *"For our struggle is not against flesh and blood, but against the rulers, against the authorities, against the powers of this dark world and against the spiritual forces of evil in the heavenly realms."*

These three places can be illustrated like this:

HEAVEN
Abode of God; Christ enthroned
Angels minister constantly
We're seated here with Christ
Where the will of God is never challenged

THE BATTLEGROUND
Abode of Satan and fallen angels
A SPIRITUAL BATTLEGROUND
Kingdoms of this world controlled from here
Where the will of God is always resisted

EARTH
Abode of Man; Kingdoms of this world
Angels, serving GOD and Satan, active here
The Kingdom of God is within us!
"Whatever you bind on earth is bound in heaven"

We'll spend a full week thinking about this together, because when you grasp the meaning of all this, your prayer life will gain new importance. From now on, understand that the Kingdom of Heaven is made real on the earth through us.

On the one hand, because we have become the children of the King, His Kingdom is in us. Therefore, we carry with us the Kingdom of Heaven on the earth.

On the other hand, Satan reigns over all the kingdoms of this world: *"Again, the devil took him to a very high mountain and showed him all the kingdoms of the world and their splendor"* (Matthew 4:8).

You spent your former life living under Satan's power. All his "kingdoms" are, in reality, prison cells. You were his prisoner! Your values, your habits, and your actions were formed while under his domination. You have now become part of a supernatural Kingdom. You are able to live in it, to hear and see and speak and feel things you have never experienced until now!

It's my prayer that as we spend these next weeks together you will recognize that being part of the Kingdom of Heaven calls for a radical shift in your lifestyle. Nothing can ever be the same for you! You have become a child of God, a member of the Kingdom, a servant of Christ. You will discover new ways of loving and laughing and speaking in the Kingdom of Heaven!

THE "KINGDOM OF HEAVEN" IS ALSO CALLED "THE KINGDOM OF GOD"

The terms are interchangeable. Where God reigns, it's "heaven." The Kingdom of Heaven brings the powerful activity of God to the earth. Jesus said, *"As you go, preach this message: 'The kingdom of heaven is near.' Heal the sick, raise the dead, cleanse those who have leprosy, drive out demons. Freely you have received, freely give"* (Matthew 10:7-8).

As a citizen of the Kingdom of God, one of your main tasks is to bring the power of heaven to those who live around you. The Christ Who now dwells in you will reach out to bless others using His power.

Jesus' final words in Matthew make this truth very clear. *"All authority in heaven and on earth has been given to me. Therefore go and make disciples of all nations, baptizing them in the name of the Father and of the Son and of the Holy Spirit, and teaching them to obey everything I have commanded you. And surely I will be with you always, to the very end of the age."*

When you became a citizen of the Kingdom of God, you also became an agent of the King. The power of God works in you to touch others because His presence is with you always.

Before Christ came to you, did you ever imagine that your life would become so significant? God works through you to bring heaven's authority to your closest friends, your relatives, and to people you have not yet met! God will use you as an instrument of His love. You will discover His power flowing through you to others! You are a link between the realm of heaven and the physical realm on earth. *Isn't that wonderful?*

Week 2, Day 2
This Unit: Kingdom Lifestyles
This Week: Let's Take a Tour
Today: Heaven

Read 2 Corinthians 12:2-4

In Acts 14:19-20, we learn that Paul was stoned and left for dead. As his companions prayed, not only was he revived, but he left 24 hours later for his next appointment. Only the power of God could have restored him! I believe it was an event similar to this he is remembering in the passage you have just read. He speaks of being "caught up to the third heaven."

The things Paul saw were too wonderful to talk about, and he was ready to return there. He described his desire to return there in Philippians 1:21, 23, *"For to me, to live is Christ and to die is gain . . . . I am torn between the two: I desire to depart and be with Christ, which is better by far; . . ."*

You see heaven is the location of the throne of God. In Revelation 4:1, 2, 8, John writes: *"After this I looked, and there before me was a door standing open in heaven. And the voice I had first heard speaking to me like a trumpet said, 'Come up here . . . .' At once I was in the Spirit, and there before me was a throne in heaven with some-one sitting on it . . . ."* John sees angels bowing down before the throne and saying, *"Holy, holy, holy is the Lord God Almighty, who was, and is, and is to come."* In Revelation 5:6, Jesus is described as the Lamb of God, standing in the center of the throne.

HEAVEN IS YOUR FINAL HOME!

After Paul visited heaven, he desired to depart from this life and go there. In 1 Corinthians 2:9 he writes, *"No eye has seen, no ear has heard, no mind has conceived what God has prepared for those who love him."*

Mrs. Lee, a Singaporean, said to me: "Please tell me about the United States. My husband and I are going to live there. What are the people like? What kind of food do you enjoy?" Her eyes were shining with excitement as we talked. *She wanted to know about where she was going!* Since the Kingdom of God now exists in heaven, the Bible makes many references to it. Today, you are going to take a peek at what's ahead of *you!*

 Look up the scriptures below:

Genesis 21:17: Where was God as Hagar's child cried?

_____

Who brought God's response to Hagar?

_____

Genesis 28:12: How does this scripture show a connection between the heaven and earth?

_____

2 Chronicles 7:14: Where is God when He hears our prayers of confession? How does He respond?

These verses show a clear connection between heaven and earth. When we pray, we are communicating all the way to God's throne. Since there is such a special connection between God and us, learning to pray is important!

Are you imagining that you cannot know anything at all about heaven until you die? You are thinking, "Paul had a very special experience."

Read carefully Ephesians 1:18-21: *"I pray also that the eyes of your heart may be enlightened in order that you may know the hope to which he has called you . . . and his incomparably great power for us who believe. That power is like the working of his mighty strength, which he exerted in Christ when he raised him from the dead and seated him at his right hand in the heavenly realms, far above all rule and authority, power and dominion, and every title that can be given, not only in the present age but also in the one to come."*

Now, here's the good news for *you*. Ephesians 2:6 says, *"And God raised us up with Christ and seated us with him in the heavenly realms in Christ Jesus."* Colossians 3:1 adds, *"Since, then, you have been raised with Christ, set your hearts on things above, where Christ is seated at the right hand of God."*

As far as God is concerned, the moment you prayed to receive Christ as your Lord, you were admitted into the heavenly realms. You can come and go from there any time you desire. It's like having an open telephone line that is never disconnected!

A lot of Christians you will meet don't understand that. As a result, they don't bother to communicate with the Lord Jesus. Paul said in 1 Thessalonians 5:17, *"pray continually."* You don't have to be in some building with stained glass walls to reach heaven! In the world of the supernatural, you are located there at this very moment. In Jude 20 we read, *"But you, dear friends, build yourselves up in your most holy faith and pray in the Holy Spirit."*

Some years ago I met Corrie Ten Boom, author of *The Hiding Place*. She was a very old woman then and had spent terrible years in a concentration camp. During her sorrow, she learned much about being in constant touch with Christ in prayer. As we sat visiting, her lips often moved. I thought it might be a habit of aged people who mouth the words they hear being spoken — but she didn't seem to be repeating what I was saying. Finally I gently said, "Miss Corrie, I see your lips moving. Is there something you want to say to me?" She replied in her Dutch accent, "Ach! You must forgive an old voman. I vas just talking to our Lord about dis lovely talk ve are having."

Your greatest privilege as a resident of the Kingdom of God is that you are already "seated with Christ" in heaven. "Set your heart on things above." Keep the line open at all times.

HOW TO PRAY FOR AN HOUR A DAY

Are you thinking, *"That's impossible! I don't know anyone who does that! That's ridiculous!"* Don't say that until you try it. Here's how: Spend 10 minutes in each of six areas: (1) Worship the Lord. Mediate on Psalm 40 and sing praise songs aloud; (2) Pray for your pastor, church, and fellow group members; (3) Pray for your government; (4) Pray for friends who don't know Christ as their Savior; (5) Pray for family members; (6) Pray for yourself. Give it a try!

Week 2, Day 3
This Unit: Kingdom Lifestyles
This Week: Let's Take a Tour
Today: The Battleground

Read Revelation 12:7-8; Ephesians 6:12; Romans 8:38-39

"And there was war in heaven . . . ." This passage is not talking about the third heaven that Paul saw where God resides and rules. It's referring to a place where spiritual battles occur.

It's important for you to understand that the battleground is not the place Jesus referred to as *hell*, the place where those who die without accepting Christ will spend eternity (Matthew 10:28). Rather, it is the place where spiritual battles are constantly taking place, the battleground for "principalities and powers" (Eph. 6:12).

Let's look at the Scriptures that will help us see when this battleground was created. It began when Lucifer, one of the highest angels in heaven, decided to become equal with God. Millenniums ago, this conflict took place:

> *"How you have fallen from heaven, O morning star, son of the dawn! You have been cast down to the earth, you who once laid low the nations! You said in your heart, 'I will ascend to heaven; I will raise my throne above the stars of God; I will sit enthroned on the mount of assembly, on the utmost heights of the sacred mountain. I will ascend above the tops of the clouds; I will make myself like the Most High.' But you are brought down to the grave, to the depths of the pit."* (Isaiah 14:12-15).

EVIL IS ALWAYS ROOTED IN SAYING "I WILL"

This was the pride-filled comment of Satan as he chose to rebel against God. Pride and rebellion against authority — these are the marks of the evil one. Wherever you see them, you see his work!

Along with him were *"the angels who did not keep their positions of authority but abandoned their own home,"* mentioned in Jude 6 and 2 Peter 2:4. It was at that time, before God created the world, that this battleground was formed. Before then there was no conflict and therefore no need for a battleground. The angels who chose to follow Satan are described in Revelation 12:7-9 as assisting Satan in warfare and are to be cast into hell.

GOD'S ANGELS PASS THROUGH THIS BATTLEGROUND

In Genesis 28:12, Jacob *"saw a stairway resting on the earth, with its top reaching to heaven, and the angels of God were ascending and descending on it."* They come to minister to members of the Kingdom of God on this earth, and sometimes they must do battle on the battleground to get through to us.

This is described for us in Daniel 10:12-13. Daniel had been agonizing for three weeks in prayer, asking God for an interpretation of a vision about a great war. The angel Gabriel finally appeared and said, *"Do not be afraid, Daniel. Since the first day that you set your mind to gain understanding and to humble yourself before your God, your words were heard, and I have come in response to them. But the prince of the Persian kingdom resisted me twenty-one days. Then Michael, one of the chief princes, came to help me, because I was detained there with the king of Persia."*

As a "little child" in God's Kingdom, it is important that you quickly understand the reality of this battleground. You will be deceived if you do not realize that you have, for the first time, been released from the domination of Satan. He is not happy about it.

Peter reminds you in 1 Peter 5:8-9, *"Be self-controlled and alert. Your enemy the devil prowls around like a roaring lion looking for someone to devour. Resist him, standing firm in the faith, because you know that your brothers throughout the world are undergoing the same kind of sufferings."*

🥀 **According to 1 John 2:13 (review week 1, day 4), what must you do before you qualify to be called a "young man" in the kingdom of God? (Check proper box or boxes)**

☐ **Attend a worship service twice a month.**

☐ **Overcome the evil one.**

☐ **Try to stop my bad habits by self-discipline.**

☐ **All of the above.**

☐ **None of the above.**

If you checked the second box, you are correct. Your first objective is to enter into spiritual battle, but your own salvation is not at stake! When Jesus took your sins upon Himself at Calvary, He took all that Satan could throw at you and became the Conqueror for you. You are totally safe in Christ! His angels attend your way! Rejoice! You cannot lose your place in the Kingdom because you were *born* into it. That's an important point!

I have three sons. As their father, I cannot ever say they are not my children. Whether they "succeed" or "fail," they are always my sons. Nothing can change that. You are a child of God, and you can't be "unborn" for any reason at all.

But you *can* find a lot of unnecessary defeat if you don't know your enemy and how he functions on the battleground. As we shall see, you must become involved in spiritual warfare. When you are able to do so, you will develop into a "young man."

Here's good news: Exodus 14:14 promises us, *"The Lord will fight for you; you need only to be still."*

🥀 **According to Romans 8:38-39, what can separate us from the love of God in Christ?**

☐ **Angels and demons.**

☐ **Powers in heaven.**

☐ **Death.**

☐ **None of the above.**

Week 2, Day 4
This Unit: Kingdom Lifestyles
This Week: Let's Take a Tour
Today: The Earth

Read Genesis 1:1; Romans 8:19-23; 2 Peter 3:10-12

The opening words of the Bible read: *"In the beginning God created the heavens and the earth."* Think about it! God made the heavens and earth, the realm you and I experience through sight, sound, and touch.

The Bible tells us in Psalm 24:1, *"The earth is the Lord's, and all it contains."* Some people think that after our God created the universe that he returned to His abode in heaven and left the world to its own means. He has been very active in its affairs. We know He owns it all. He Himself said, *"Everything under heaven belongs to me"* (Job 41:11).

Since that is true, why does Romans 8:22 tell us that *"the whole creation has been groaning as in the pains of childbirth right up to the present time"*? That is a very important question for us to answer!

When God made the heavens and the earth, He chose to make Adam and his descendants (that includes you!) the caretakers of them. He told them to *"increase in number; fill the earth and subdue it. Rule over the fish of the sea and the birds of the air and over every living creature that moves on the ground"* (Genesis 1:28).

According to this scripture, what is your role in creation?

☐   **Do nothing and let God "take care" of everything.**

☐   **Control, abuse and use up the creation that God made for your own pleasure.**

☐   **Work in God's creation under God's direction as His caretaker.**

☐   **Do whatever we like with creation since God has nothing to do with everyday life.**

SATAN COULDN'T STAND FOR THAT!

How could Satan permit this new creature called "Man" to have such control over the world and the heavens above it? This would never do! He had the perfect scheme. He appealed to the pride within Eve and Adam. In Genesis 3:5, he tempted Eve by saying, *"For God knows that when you eat of it [that is, if you will disobey God] your eyes will be opened, and you will be like God, knowing good and evil."*

The Scriptures tell us that the first man and woman were the first to disobey God, but not the last. Every single one of us has done the same thing! We are told in Isaiah 53:6 that we are all like sheep who have gone astray. One of the greatest tragedies of history is that man, from the start, has not taken care of the heavens and the earth God entrusted to him. In every case — without exception — the goal of Satan is to destroy. In fact, one of the names given to him in Revelation 9:11 is "Destroyer." When we join Adam and Eve in disobedience, we contribute to this goal of destruction.

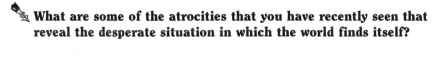

DO YOU LIKE THE SMELL OF GARBAGE?

One whiff, and you have had enough — correct? Pity this poor, suffering planet that has lived with all the human filth of the centuries. There are mountains of garbage. Both the forests and the seas are being destroyed. Yet, the ecological disasters are minor issues when compared to the massive evil deeds performed by prideful men since the beginning of time.

Think of the atrocities, the murders, the genocides, the wars, the thefts, the swindling, and the broken families and lives you personally know about. Multiply that for millenniums and into every country, and you can understand why *"The creation waits in eager expectation"* (Romans 8:19).

What are some of the atrocities that you have recently seen that reveal the desperate situation in which the world finds itself?

_____

_____

THINGS ARE NOT ALWAYS GOING TO BE LIKE THEY ARE

"The whole creation has been groaning as in the pains of childbirth" because the disobedience of man has a far-reaching impact. Disobedience destroys. Romans 8:20-23 tells us that all of creation knows that before it can be different, humankind must be different. This will happen when the "sons of God" are revealed at the end of the present age.

2 Peter 3:10-12 explains that at the end of this age, God is going to destroy everything on this planet with fire. In Revelation 21:1, John saw in a vision what would happen: *"Then I saw a new heaven and a new earth, for the first heaven and the first earth had passed away, and there was no longer any sea."* This verse paints a vivid picture of our future hope. Since that's the way things will end, we ought to live for the Kingdom of God now. Your on-going work in *The Arrival Kit* will assist you as you journey into God's Kingdom. As a Christian, you live in it right now!

Week 2, Day 5
This Unit: Kingdom Lifestyles
This Week: Let's Take a Tour
Today: Customs Inspection is Next!

Read Ephesians 2:1-6; 2 Timothy 3:2-5

My seat assignment placed me next to a young man who seemed to be very nervous. As we approached Singapore, he asked, "Is it true that they hang those who bring drugs into their country?"

"Absolutely!" I answered. "If they catch someone at the border with an illegal substance, he goes straight to prison, and if he is found guilty before the court, they hang him."

He was strangely silent. Suddenly he got up and went into the bathroom. When he came back, he had a look of relief on his face. I guessed what had happened, and said, "You got rid of something too dangerous to keep, didn't you?" He looked at me with shame and said, "You won't tell anyone, will you?"

Because of his dress, his hairstyle, and his age, he was taken aside by the Customs Inspector when we landed. He had made a very wise decision: he had gotten rid of baggage that was not permitted in the Republic he was about to enter!

For all the years we lived until we came to Christ and became sons of God, our lives were filled with the habits and values described in our two Scripture portions for today. As you think about the way you have been "programmed" in the past, are you carrying baggage that needs to be discarded?

🌹 **Read Ephesians 2:1-2. According to this teaching, whom did you serve before becoming a Christian?**

_____

🌹 **Read Ephesians 2:3. Would you agree that it is referring to your past lifestyle?**

☐ **Yes. It's not easy to admit it, but it's true.**
☐ **No.**
☐ **I have to think about that!**

Some years ago, my wife Ruth was attached to an emergency hospital team. Sometimes she went to the scene of a train wreck to help the victims. She knew what to do for them. Then one day she hit another car head on. She was badly hurt! When we got her to the hospital, she *didn't* say to the attendants, "I have a broken right arm that needs a splint, and I need an intravenous solution to keep me from going into shock." Instead, she said to the physician, *"Doctor! Help me!"*

Those who enter the Kingdom and agree with God that they are carrying "old baggage" that cannot "clear customs" get off to a good start. Don't be uncomfortable with what you are asked to do in the activity below — instead, let it be the act of a child of God who is "agreeing with God" about the past, and perhaps the present. You need to swallow your pride and say, *"Lord, I need a lot of healing. Help me!"*

 Look over this baggage list from 2 Timothy 3:2-5. Prayerfully <u>underline</u> items that were/are part of your lifestyle. As you do so, thank Him/ask Him to release you from them:

- **Lover of myself**
- **Abusive (to whom?)**
- **Without love**
- **Brutal**
- **Conceited**
- **Lover of money**
- **Unholy**
- **Without self-control**
- **Rash**

- **Boastful**
- **Ungrateful**
- **Slanderous**
- **Treacherous**
- **Proud**
- **Disobedient to parents**
- **Unforgiving (of whom?)**
- **Not a lover of good**

- **A lover of pleasure rather than a lover of God**
- **Having a form of Godliness but denying its power**

As you review what you have underlined, which ones would you say give you the most trouble *right now*? Those are the ones the evil one will use to cripple you, to rob you of your peace and your joy.

Others have come to the "entry point" of the Kingdom of God and have placed baggage just like yours on the inspection counter. Their problem, perhaps like yours, is that *they just could not find the way to dispose of it!*

Here is a prayer that you may want to learn by heart. It has great power to release you from old baggage:

> *"Lord Jesus, this baggage has been with me for a very long time. When I've tried to get rid of it before, I have always failed. I don't carry this baggage in my hands. It's deep inside me. It is as much a part of me as my skin and my bones. I am helpless before it. I want to be released from it. I confess to You that I cannot even help You with the process. I believe in You, and I believe You have the power to release me. You have come from heaven to live in my life. I now invite You to work in my life. I cannot give this baggage to You, but if You will take it from me, it is Yours! Thank you for being my Deliverer!"*

May I be transparent with you? I carried a bitterness in my heart for over 25 years against someone who had really, truly done a wrong thing to me. I wasn't just imagining it. When God finally made me see it was *baggage,* that was destroying *me,* I realized I couldn't do anything to stop the way I felt. In the dark of the night, I stretched out my hand and prayed the above prayer. I surrendered the bitterness to Him. Slowly, He removed it from me. That was 38 years ago. *He will do the same for you today!*

Week 3, Day 1
This Unit: The Kingdoms of This World
This Week: What's Old?
Today: Leaving Old Kingdoms Behind

Read Isaiah 37:15-16; 60:12; Galatians 3:22, 26-28; Philippians 3:20

Very early in the Bible, we discover kingdoms being formed. In Genesis 10:8-10 Nimrod, a "mighty hunter," was building a kingdom. We see him acting with the thirst of a hunter after the prey, conquering vast areas and people. From the beginning, the earth has fallen into the hands of greedy hunters. With a lust for control, humans have always desired to be called "King."

Satan, knowing this, has from the beginning of history manipulated people to form kingdoms. In all cases, and without any exceptions, kingdoms have been built upon greed and power.

I visited a rich man's ranch in West Texas where a huge wild game reserve had been created. He had imported animals from all over the world. The man who studied their habits said to me, "Nearly every square foot of these tens of thousands of acres is under the control of an animal, or a group of them." He pointed to a hill a mile away and said, "For example, that hill is the territory of one mountain goat. If another animal visits there, it's at the risk of its life!" I thought to myself, "There's a bit of that animal spirit in everyone!"

Satan has deliberately manipulated the development of "kingdoms" or "nations" to separate and destroy innocent people. The character for China, which means "middle kingdom," looks like this: 中 The square box in the center represents China. The line projecting from the top represents Korea; the line below, Vietnam. For the early Chinese community, the rest of the world just didn't exist!

Every nation or kingdom considers itself to be the most important of all. Those outside are called "aliens," a word describing the "alienated." They have no rights of citizenship. Some people never even stray from their "native land."

Those who put their nation before God may not bow down to an image of stone, but they break the First Commandment: "You shall have no other gods before me." Through the nationalistic worship of nations, whole generations have been maimed and slaughtered. In the twentieth century, one hundred million lives were offered on the altars of kings who were determined to rule regardless of the cost! The Jewish holocaust of this century demonstrates what can happen.

Romans 13:1-7 instructs us to submit to those in authority over us. Just as we are to be loyal citizens of our nation, there is also the need to be loyal to our citizenship in the Kingdom of God. This may be a difficult thing for you to grasp, but you might as well face it early in your Christian life: *When you swear allegiance to God, you must set aside your loyalty to a culture created by Satan.*

Embedded within every nation is a unique culture. It entwines us like a rope, to bind us until we are not free. Many things found in a culture are positive. For example, in some cultures the divorce rate is only 2% because entire families surround a couple with a marriage problem and help them solve it. Compare this with other cultures

30

where the divorce rate often equals or exceeds the marriage rate!

Some aspects of cultures are *not* neutral. They are demonic. When a culture teaches its children to worship idols, for example, *it is evil*. When a culture permits promiscuity and drugs, *it is evil*. In the United States' constitution, there is a phrase: "We hold these truths to be self-evident . . ." Such a comment may become a statement rejecting the reign of God over it. It may allow a society to look at itself and say, *"If something seems right to us, it is right for us to do it."* Our loyalty must be to Christ even when it conflicts with our culture.

According to Isaiah 37:15-16, who has final power and control over what happens to the kingdoms of this earth?

- ☐ **The man, or men, who reign over a nation.**
- ☐ **Satan.**
- ☐ **God.**
- ☐ **All of the above.**
- ☐ **None of the above.**

We all carry the indelible marks of our "kingdoms," for either good or bad. Therefore, in the days ahead, you will examine the values which have saturated you from childhood.

According to Isaiah 60:12, what happens to every nation or kingdom that will not serve God?

It will _____

Rewrite Galatians 3:22 in your own words:

_____

_____

_____

Ultimately, the nation that rejects God's rule over it comes to ruin. History is loaded with examples of powerful nations that disintegrated!

According to Galatians 3:26-28, why do we as believers refuse to discriminate between brothers and sisters who are "Jew or Greek?"

- ☐ **We set aside our national costumes to clothe ourselves with Christ.**
- ☐ **Our ethnic and cultural backgrounds have no further significance.**
- ☐ **Both of the above.**
- ☐ **None of the above.**

Week 3, Day 2
This Unit: The Kingdoms of This World
This Week: What's Old?
Today: Who's Running the Kingdom?

Read Luke 4:5-8

Satan was really frightened when Jesus was born, so he did his best to have this baby destroyed. Satan worked through kings. For example, Jesus' family had to hide away in Egypt for a time because king Herod ordered all the young boys in his region to be killed (Matthew 2:13-23). When Jesus was fully grown, Satan worked through religious leaders, trying to inspire them to murder Jesus (Matthew 12:14; Mark 3:6).

Satan was most threatened by what Jesus preached: *"Repent, for the kingdom of heaven is near"* (Matthew 4:17). Having controlled the kingdoms of this world for centuries, the Devil's power was now being challenged by the offer of a new Kingdom!

Satan had developed powerful supernatural systems, with fallen angels serving as controlling "princes" over every kingdom (Daniel 10:20-21). Satan and his fallen angles worked to block the knowledge of God. If Jesus established His Kingdom, Satan would lose his power. His "kingdoms" were actually *prison systems* to capture mankind. All were designed to keep men from thinking about God.

Following His public baptism by John the Baptist, Jesus was led by the Holy Spirit into the wilderness to be tempted by the Devil. From God's viewpoint, this was a positive test. From the Devil's standpoint, it gave him an opportunity to try and control Jesus. If he could do so, God's power could be broken.

How could Satan show Jesus all the kingdoms of this world in an instant of time?

- ☐ This is a supernatural event and cannot be explained in natural terms.
- ☐ It indicates Satan's power over time and space.
- ☐ Both of the above.
- ☐ I cannot come to any conclusion about this. I will discuss it with my mentor.

In Luke 4:6, Satan offered Jesus two values from the kingdoms of this world. What were they?

1. _____

2. _____

Satan used these two values (authority and splendor) because they always appeal to the primary desires of human beings. *Would Jesus yield to the temptation of these two values?* That was the big question!

Satan offered an exchange: all *he* controlled for the right to control *Jesus*. It didn't work! It is important for us to understand the reply of Jesus. We are not to worship the kingdoms of this world, or *anything inside of them.* Two of the things most valued by humans are control over others (authority) and recognition from others (splendor).

SATAN OFFERS FALSE VALUES TO EVERYONE!

Think about your own set of values. Has Satan penetrated your value system through his temptations? Whatever Satan can offer to stop you from worshipping God is fair game for him! What do *you* desire *so much* that you are willing to put Christ's Kingdom into second — or third or last — place in your priority system? Sometimes those who *enter* the Kingdom of God continue seeking personal power or glory. *It's so deeply ingrained into us that we have a tough time breaking its hold.*

Study the list of values below. Select the one you would rank first in your present lifestyle. Write a "1" in the blank next to it. Next, select the value you would rank least important, and write "18" next to it. Then rank the rest by selecting the next highest as "2" and then the next lowest as "17", etc., until each item has been given a separate ranking.

(This exercise will take some time. If you need to do so, come back to this tomorrow and rethink your answers. You can complete the final day of this unit on one of the two "off days" left in the week. Take this ranking seriously. We will refer to this page often in the following units.)

MY VALUE SYSTEM, PART 1	
PRIORITY	VALUE
_____	Being prosperous, wealthy
_____	Doing exciting things
_____	Accomplishing something big
_____	Living without conflict
_____	Feeling equal with others
_____	Making my family secure
_____	Free to make my own choices
_____	Being happy, contented
_____	Avoiding inner conflicts
_____	Having close friends
_____	Being safe from crime
_____	Enjoying life (travel, movies, etc.)
_____	Doing the will of God
_____	Having self-respect, self-esteem
_____	Being recognized and admired
_____	Closeness, intimacy with others
_____	Making good decisions
_____	Desire for power

Week 3, Day 3
This Unit: The Kingdoms of This World
This Week: What's Old?
Today: Solomon's Conclusions

Read Ecclesiastes 1:1-2; 2:4-11; 12:13

When Solomon became king of Israel, God gave him *"a wise and discerning heart, so that there will never have been anyone like you, nor will there ever be."* (1 Kings 3:12). At the end of his life, Solomon wrote the book of Ecclesiastes, a pessimistic verdict about life in the kingdoms of this world.

In Ecclesiastes 2:3, he describes how he came to his conclusion. He explains that he experienced all the activities of life with his mind guiding him with wisdom. He says, "I wanted to see what was worthwhile for men to do under heaven during the few days of their lives."

He had the power and the wealth to try everything. He had many wives, the finest houses, and many beautiful things. Solomon tested all the values we think make life worth living. What he concluded is very significant!

Satan is no fool. If he offered most of us a lifestyle of lust and immorality, thievery and violence, we would turn away from him. Therefore, he offers *seemingly harmless values*, promising they will bring us happiness. We are deceived by him and spend our lives seeking happiness in all the wrong ways.

At the end of Ecclesiastes, Solomon comes to a single conclusion about what really makes life worthwhile. Before we look at it, let's trace a few of the values he tested:

In Ecclesiastes 2:4-11, which of the following values did Solomon test?

☐ **Being prosperous, wealthy.**
☐ **Doing the will of God.**
☐ **Accomplishing something big.**
☐ **Doing exciting things.**

What was his conclusion in verse 11?
(Use your own words for your answer:)

_____

_____

In Ecclesiastes 12:13, what was his final conclusion?

_____

_____

_____

_____

34

How do you think Solomon would have ranked these values at the end of his life? (Choose two: the one you think he would rank "1", and the one he might rank "18" from the list below.)

Satan entices us to adopt every value in the list, except for one. *Doing the will of God* is the only value that belongs in the Kingdom of God, not in the kingdoms of this world. All the others are, as Solomon said, "Meaningless! Meaningless! Utterly meaningless! *Everything* is meaningless."

Is this too radical a thought for you? If so, scan the list. Ask yourself, "If this value were not a part of my life, how miserable would I be?" Examples: "I would enjoy living with conflict. I don't need to feel safe from crime. I don't have to enjoy life. I don't need close friends. I don't have to be prosperous."

As you thought about the very negative comments made above, did you feel a sense of threat or fear? In reality, do you fear *not* being safe from crime, or your family being *insecure*? Of course. We all do!

Often our fears control our every action. They are the bars of our prison cells. For example, a lady grew up in poverty. She was so afraid she would be poor in her later years that she worked day and night to save money. As a result, she had no time for her children's needs. They grew up without her love or her time. When she finally retired, she still feared poverty, even though she had a large savings account. In her old age, no one cared about her. She had allowed her fear of poverty to destroy the meaning of life. She had no friends. This is a sad example of Satan's plan. He wants us to focus on false values. He blinds us to the results of spending our lives chasing after things that bring no peace to our lives.

SOLOMON'S VALUE SYSTEM

PRIORITY   VALUE

____   Being prosperous, wealthy

____   Having close friends

____   Doing exciting things

____   Being safe from crime

____   Accomplishing something big

____   Enjoying life

____   Living without conflict

____   Doing the will of God

____   Feeling equal with others

____   Having self-respect, self-esteem

____   Making his family secure

____   Being recognized and admired

____   Free to make his own choices

____   Closeness, intimacy with others

____   Being happy, contented

____   Making good decisions

____   Avoiding inner conflicts

____   Desire for power

Week 3, Day 4
This Unit: The Kingdoms of This World
This Week: What's Old?
Today: Who Controls You?

Read 1 John 5:19, Romans 6:20-23

The word for *"control"* used in both these verses refers to Satan's power *"spread over"* the world. In both passages, we are told unbelievers have no freedom. *All* unbelievers live under the domination of Satan. And from time to time Christians may also succumb to Satan's control.

One of Jesus' disciples was named Peter. His courage to stand up for Jesus faded when he was alone in a hostile crowd. He denied his Lord three times in one night. When we find ourselves controlled by Satan's crowd, we have decisions to make.

Satan usually controls people by putting them under the control of others. For example, a 55-year-old Chinese lady explained to her cell group that she could not make a public confession of her faith in Christ because she did not want to offend her mother who worshiped idols. Therefore, she kept her Christianity a secret for several years. Not offending her mother was a higher priority to her than publicly proclaiming her faith in Christ. She did not yet understand Jesus' words in Luke 9:26: "If anyone is ashamed of me and my words, the Son of Man will be ashamed of him when he comes in his glory and in the glory of the Father and of the holy angels."

She had spent her life pleasing her mother, who totally controlled her. In reality, Satan's control had blinded her mother to God's love for over 75 years! The daughter's silence hindered God's grace from coming to her own mother, who was facing eternal separation from God in a place Jesus called "Hell."

Someone has said, "We all look over our shoulders to see if we are pleasing people who are watching what we do." These "special people" in our lives may be parents, a spouse, an employer, someone you are dating, or a gang member. If Satan controls these people, then entering the Kingdom of God may cause you to face opposition. How will you handle it?

In which of the following situations would fear of rejection cause you to be silent and not act like a citizen of God's kingdom? (Check proper box or boxes)

☐ **You are in a group desiring to party in a way not appropriate for a Christian.**

☐ **You have taken over a business with shady practices, which you are told to continue.**

☐ **You are with old friends who do not know you have accepted Christ as your Lord.**

☐ **All of the above.**

☐ **None of the above.**

You have lived for years with God being unimportant to you. Your mind has never been exposed to the supernatural work of God before, and Satan has silently controlled your every thought. Much of his control over you is through people. Who are they? How do they control you? How can you be set free from obeying them rather than your new Lord?

Even more important, how can you influence them for Christ, rather than allowing their influence over you to place you temporarily under Satan's control?

Who owns you?

Who owns your body?

Who owns your mind?

Who owns your emotions?

Many centuries ago, Augustine was a wild young man who partied and consorted with prostitutes. After his conversion, one of them caught him by the arm and invited him to her room. He said, "I am sorry. The Augustine you know is dead. This is a new Augustine, and you do not know what sort of man he is."

You will face situations where you will want to respond in a similar manner. The Holy Spirit will show you how to do it at the proper time. Make a decision NOW to be a public Christian rather than a secret one. Choose not to be a *closet* Christian but an *exposed* Christian.

Now that you have chosen to follow Jesus, Satan will try to control you through people you do not want to offend. *Who are those people? How will you deal with them?* Perhaps you will benefit by sharing your feelings about all this with your mentor or your cell group. Ask for support and prayer!

Week 3, Day 5
This Unit: The Kingdoms of This World
This Week: What's Old?
Today: The End of the Kingdoms

Read Daniel 2:44; Deuteronomy 5:8-9

While the primary way God speaks to us is through the Bible, He does speak in other ways. This Scripture in Daniel is part of a story of a wicked king named Nebuchadnezzar who received a message from God through a dream. The prophet Daniel interpreted the dream for him and described a time still in the future when Satan's "kingdoms of this world" will be replaced:

> "... the God of heaven will set up a kingdom that will never be destroyed, nor will it be left to another people. It will crush all those kingdoms and bring them to an end, but it will itself endure forever."

You can discover many things in your Bible about the time when Jesus returns to the earth to reign as King of kings. The important thing for you to remember is that you don't have to wait for His Kingdom to appear. Jesus said in Luke 17:20: *"the kingdom of God is within you."* As Christians live in the kingdoms of this world, Christ's Kingdom lives within them! While unbelievers worship the gods of this world, we worship the true God. We have put away old gods to focus our attention exclusively on Jesus Christ.

Since we know that the possessions, powers, and pleasures of this age are "gods" to many, how should we value them? Some people say we should have nothing at all to do with "worldly" things. They suggest we should live simply, reject all pleasures, and refuse to have anything to do with entertainment.

On the other hand, there are those who say we should expect God to make us rich and prosperous, and we should enjoy the kingdoms of this world to the fullest. Some even go so far as to teach that prosperity is the proof that you are a Christian — that God rewards those He loves by making them rich.

As you live in Christ's Kingdom, how *should* you deal with possessions? First of all, they should not be worshiped. Often an automobile, a house, or even a hobby can become an idol.

According to Deuteronomy 5:8, what forms can idols take?

- ☐ Anything in Heaven above.
- ☐ Anything on the earth beneath.
- ☐ Anything in the waters below.
- ☐ All of the above.
- ☐ None of the above.

In Asia, idols of wood, metal, and porcelain are frequently seen. Snakes are worshiped in temples. There are many idols, and each one breaks the First Commandment: "You shall have no other gods before me." Thus, when an idol-worshipping family comes to Jesus, the entire cell group often helps destroy them. As idols are being burned, the group sings praise songs to Jesus.

It is obvious that a true Christian does not preserve old idols — *but does that always happen?* Sometimes the "idols" are not called *Hanemun* or *Quan Yin*. For some, idols are called *Honda*, or *Furniture*, or *Tennis*, or *Luxury Home*, or even *Food* (Phil. 3:19). Anything that adversely affects our relationship with God is an idol.

We can also make idols out of people we love. In my opinion, this was a problem in Abraham's life. He loved Isaac so much that the boy became an idol. It was for this reason that God told him to sacrifice his son. It was a painful time for Abraham! He had to decide whether he should worship God or his son. He made the right choice — and in effect God said, "Abraham, you don't have to sacrifice your son. I just wanted you to quit worshipping him. He was becoming an idol in your life."

Do you have a person in your life as important to you as God? If so, you worship an idol. Even your own child can become an idol.

Here's a tough question for you to answer:

What is the difference between a normal interest in someone or something and he/she/it becoming your god?

_____

_____

_____

_____

Take some time right now to pray about the gods, the idols, the loved ones, or possessions in your life which may be robbing God of your total devotion. He has said, *"You shall not bow down to them or worship them; for I, the Lord your God, am a jealous God."* Get rid of the old. Live in the Kingdom with a new commitment!

Week 4, Day 1
This Unit: The Kingdoms of This World
This Week: What's New?
Today: All About "Oikos"

Read Ephesians 2:19-22; 1 Corinthians 12:12-21

Do you remember Ephesians 2:19-22? We meditated on it in the material for Week 1, Day 1. We are going to think about a great truth found in verse 19, where we learn that we are *"members of God's household."* In the original language of Paul, the word for *household* is *oikos*.

Remember the word *oikos*. We will use it over and over during your equipping journey. (We'll also discover this week there are two special words which belong to the *oikos* family.)

An *oikos* is a small group of people who have a very special relationship to one another. They spend at least a total of one hour every week talking to each other. That makes them an *oikos*, a *household*. It may surprise you to learn that most of us have a very small *oikos*! We really don't spend much time actually *talking* much to other people. We know many more people than we talk to for a full hour, spread in minutes here and there over seven days.

You have always had an *oikos* in your life. There have always been special people you considered "family," even when you did not have a blood relationship with them.

🪶 **List at least four people you talk to for a total of sixty minutes every seven days. If there are more than four, put two to a line:**

_____   _____

_____   _____

🪶 **According to 1 Corinthians 12:13, what has the Holy Spirit done for you?**

☐   **He baptized me into the body of Christ.**

☐   **He made it possible for me to drink His Spirit.**

☐   **Both of the above.**

☐   **None of the above.**

When the Holy Spirit observed you praying to Jesus and asking Him to forgive you of your sins, He immediately did something *for you*! He baptized you into the body of Christ. The word baptize means to *"fully immerse."* Sometimes people talk about deciding to "join a church." They do not understand that the Holy Spirit has already joined them to the body of Christ! And since the Holy Spirit has *already* joined you to the body of Christ, it is important for you to choose a local church (body of believers) and to become accountable in a cell group. This is the reality of belonging to the *body of Jesus Christ*. You see, a *body* is not an organization; it is an *organism*. It connects the members to one another as a human body has hands, feet, etc. That "body of Christ" in the Bible is also called an *oikos*.

Households are never large. They are made up of a small group of people who become very close to one another, and who care for each other. Sometimes we call an *oikos* a "Basic Christian Community," a "cell group," or a "shepherd group." Whatever it is called, the Holy Spirit forms it and makes it an intimate family, a "body," with each person attached to the rest. Typically, one *oikos* will comprise not more than 15 persons. After that, the "family" becomes too large to spend quality time with one another.

In Matthew 28:18-20, Jesus told us that after the Holy Spirit has baptized us into His body, we are to make a special testimony for others to observe. It is done by being fully immersed in water, telling the world you have died to an old lifestyle and have been *raised in newness of life*. (You can read more about this in Romans 6:1-10.) If you have not yet been baptized as Jesus commanded, you should do so as quickly as possible. Discuss this with your cell leader.

In your *oikos*, you will observe a special meal called "The Lord's Supper" (see 1 Corinthians 11:23-25) The earliest Christians called it a "Love Feast." It is a wonderful meal. For more help in understanding its meaning and place in your *oikos*, talk to your mentor in your next get-together, or to one of the "Fathers" (see pages 14-15).

Can you remember the names of those present in your last *oikos* (cell group) gathering? (Pray a blessing for each one you can recall!)

Dear Brothers and Sisters of Mine,

Come and share My Meal!

We're meeting in My honor. On the night before I died for you, I had a meal with My disciples. I told them to remember my death by that meal. Every time they ate it, they remembered that I died for them. Now that you are a part of the Father's family, I want you to remember what I have done for you by eating this meal. Share it with the members of your cell group, knowing I am in your midst.

No one has ever deserved to take part in this meal. Remember that fact!

As far as our Father is concerned, you will also be remembering the mess your life was in, and how I dealt with it when I took your place on the cross. He says to you as you partake, "You are my child. I love you. I am proud of you!" Tell Him you love him.

— Jesus

(Adapted from *Ka Mate Ka Ora*, © Houhanga Rongo, Howick, Auckland, NZ)

Week 4, Day 2
This Unit: The Kingdoms of This World
This Week: What's New?
Today: Your New Responsibility

Read Genesis 4:8-10; Galatians 5:25-6:4; Acts 5:1-11

Cain murdered his brother, Abel. When God asked Cain where Abel was, Cain asked, "Am I my brother's keeper?" Cain's jealousy of his brother caused him to be a murderer. Before that jealousy developed, Cain had a more basic problem: *he did not feel responsible for his brother!*

A Polish sociologist examined a society of people for many months. Her report revealed that humans tend to place people into three groups. She called the first group the "People People," those individuals we accept as equal and desire to have relationships with.

The second group she called the "Machine People," those we are polite to because *we need them to service our needs.* This group may include a repairman, a household servant, a cashier, or a waitress.

The final group she called the "Landscape People," the hundreds of individuals we pass by each day on the streets, the elevators, etc. We have no interest in them at all. They are totally unimportant to us. Newspapers constantly repeat stories of murders, muggings, and rapes taking place on crowded streets with uninterested people watching the episode.

To belong to God's *oikos* means that you will accept those in the church and your cell group as "People People." Yesterday, we read this verse: *"The eye cannot say to the hand, 'I don't need you!' And the head cannot say to the feet, 'I don't need you!'"* (1 Cor. 12:21). True followers of Jesus become responsible for those around them because Jesus lives within them.

This boy played in the mud. He just arrived at your front door and wants to enter. What response would you probably make to him?

☐   "Come back when you're clean!"

☐   "Just come in. The mud doesn't matter."

☐   "Stay there! I'll come and clean you up!"

☐   "Why don't you stop your bad habits?"

According to Galatians 6:1, what would be a Christian response?

In your cell group, you leave a bag with your identity cards and some money on your chair at break time. The group members are informally visiting together, getting refreshments. When you return to your seat, you check your bag. The money has been stolen! No one from outside the group has come into the room. You are aware there is a thief in your group. *What would you do?*

🖋 **If the solutions below don't fit your answer, write it in the space provided:**

- ☐ **I would leave the group and never return.**
- ☐ **I would tell the group about the theft.**
- ☐ **I would remain silent and begin to pray for guidance about how to help the thief.**
- ☐ **I would ask for everyone to be searched.**
- ☐ _____

Do you recognize how our value systems would influence our responses to this situation? Those who fear being around thieves would *leave* the group. Those who wish to bring disgrace on offenders would *inform* the group. Those who want justice would demand a *body* search be done. Those who feel the person is *more important than the theft* would respond in a different manner, more appropriate to the Galatians passage.

We never know how we will assume responsibility for others until we are faced with the need to do so. Our challenge is in deciding whether we will handle the situation according to Satan's value system or God's value system.

Do you remember when the Pharisees brought the woman taken in adultery to Jesus? (John 8:3-11). They wanted to stone her! Jesus' value system was very different. He forgave her and told her to go and sin no more.

Ananias and Sapphira (Acts 5:1-11) tried to live by non-Kingdom values. They wanted to "look good" to the others in the Body of Christ, but in reality they did not care about the needs of their brothers and sisters in Christ. They falsified the contributions and "lied to the Holy Spirit." It was their way of saying, "Am I my brother's keeper?" As a result, they both died instantly. The amount of money they gave was not the issue. Their lack of caring for the needs of their fellow Christians was their problem.

The value of your brother or sister in your cell group is something to ponder over. Sooner or later, the "warts and pimples" will begin to show on each person. That is not the time to decide their value. Do it now.

P. S. Notice in Acts 4:35 the believers did not give funds directly to one another. Instead, they put them "at the apostle's feet" for distribution. Typically, it is not good to help someone in your cell group directly. Sometimes being responsible for your fellow Christian requires much more than money! There may be more to a situation than you know. Get the church leadership involved.

Week 4, Day 3
This Unit: The Kingdoms of This World
This Week: What's New?
Today: "Pais" — Son, or Servant?

Read Matthew 12:18; 14:1-2; 1 John 4:13 and 17

Today, we're going to have a Bible study about a word that reveals a significant truth. This word, *PAIS*, is the Greek word translated in your Bible as child, and also as son. Fix that fact in your mind: *PAIS* can mean both *child* and *son*. Let's examine some examples of that:

In Matthew 17:18, Scripture says: *". . . and the PAIS was healed from that moment."* The King James version translates that verse this way: *"and the child was cured from that very hour."* But the New American Standard Version is different. It reads, *"and the boy was cured at once."*

You see, in these translations *PAIS* is translated both *child* and *boy*, inter-changeably. If you are a *PAIS* of God, you are a *child*, or a *son*, of God. The word is used to describe a relationship between a father and his son. *That's the point: PAIS describes a relationship!* It is used to explain that our significance is in who we *are* — in our *sonship. PAIS* describes a relationship!

Now, let's look at another use of the word, causing an amazing truth to be seen. Look at Matthew 14:1-2. A totally different word in English is used to translate *PAIS* here — a most unexpected word! *"At that time Herod the tetrarch heard the news about Jesus, and said to his servants (PAIS), . . ."*

Here is a new use of the word *PAIS*. In the first example, it meant *child*, or *son*. Now, in this second example, it means *servant*! How can this be?

This double use of the word is really a key to understanding an important truth. *The significance of what we do is the result of who we are.* To be a *son* or a *child* of God is to automatically become a *servant* of God.

Let's look at four instances where the King James Version and the New American Standard Bible use *PAIS* to bring out both meanings:

Acts 3:13 is presented below, first in the King James Version, then in the New American Standard Bible:

"God . . . hath glorified his *Son (PAIS)* Jesus; . . ."
"God . . . has glorified His *servant (PAIS)* Jesus, . . ."

The word *PAIS* has two interchangeable meanings. Jesus the *Son* was Jesus the *Servant*; to be a *servant* was to be a *son*!

Acts 3:26 is presented below, first in the King James Version, then in the New American Standard Bible:

"God, having raised up his *Son (PAIS)* Jesus, . . ."
"God, raised up His *Servant (PAIS)*, [Jesus], . . ."

In Acts 4:27 and in Acts 4:30, once again these two versions use different English words for *PAIS*:

"Thy holy child *[son] (PAIS)* Jesus, . . ."
"Thy holy *servant (PAIS)* Jesus, . . ."

Consider now the most important of all the *PAIS* passages. It is in Isaiah 42:1, an Old Testament passage, where the coming of Jesus is predicted:

THE CHILDREN OF GOD ARE ALL SERVANTS OF GOD

"Behold, My Servant, whom I uphold; My chosen one in whom My soul delights. I have put My Spirit upon Him; He will bring forth justice to the nations."

This Old Testament passage was written in *Hebrew*. In Matthew 12:18, that passage was quoted using *Greek* in place of the *Hebrew* of Isaiah. As you may have guessed, *PAIS* was used:

"Behold, My Servant (PAIS) whom I have chosen; . . ."

Here it is properly translated *servant*, not *son*!

Each of the passages we have been looking at refers to our Lord Jesus Christ. His very nature as the *Son* of God was to be the *Servant* of God. It is impossible to even think of Jesus, the *Son* of God, without also remembering He was the *Servant* of God.

God declared that Jesus would come as a Servant. The entire book of Mark was written to describe Jesus as the *Servant*. He Himself said in Luke 22:27, *"I am among you as one who serves."* In Matthew 20:28, He stated that He *"did not come to be served, but to serve, and to give His life as a ransom for many."*

The very nature of God's Son, Jesus, was to be a Servant — and this is also true of us as well. *Sonship makes us servants!*

Why is this true? Because the *significance of what we do is the result of who we are.*

Consider these statements found in 1 John 4:13 and 17 (NASB):

"By this we know that we abide in Him and He in us, because He has given us of His Spirit . . . as He is, so also are we in this world."

When God adopted us as His children, He placed within our lives a brand new nature. *The Spirit of Christ* was planted inside of us. That, you see, makes us *significant*! Imagine how precious we become to our Heavenly Father after He has planted the Spirit of Jesus inside of us! That fact separates us forever from Adam's children.

Do you see the point? Jesus, the *Son* and the *Servant* of God, has given us His Spirit. If His Spirit lives within us, our new nature is going to be His nature — and His nature is that of a *Servant*. Being a child of God means we are automatically His servant. It is no option. *In the Kingdom of God, being a servant is a lifestyle.*

Week 4, Day 4
This Unit: The Kingdoms of This World
This Week: What's New?
Today: "Oikonomos"

Read Luke 12:42; 1 Corinthians 4:1-2; 1 Peter 4:10; Malachi 3:8

Yesterday, we learned that a child of God is automatically a servant of God. Do you remember the Greek word that revealed this? (Write the word below. Refer to pages 44-45 if you need help to find the answer.)

THE WORD IS __ __ __ __ .

Being a servant means learning to think in a new way about assets. The Greek words *oikonomos* and *oikodomeo* are both members of the *oikos* family tree. Learning their meanings will help us discover what our ministry involves. Today, we'll consider the first of these words.

Oikonomos is translated "manager" or "steward" in Luke 12:42. This person is described as one the master has assigned to meet the needs of his household *(oikos)* servants. The *oikonomos* gives the servants their food allowances at the proper time. Obviously, the *oikonomos* does not use his funds to do this. The only resources he has available is what the master has entrusted to him. The *oikonomos* cannot *distribute* food unless the master first *provides* the food.

Let's diagram this:

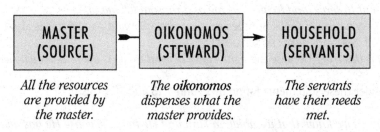

MASTER (SOURCE)	OIKONOMOS (STEWARD)	HOUSEHOLD (SERVANTS)
All the resources are provided by the master.	*The oikonomos dispenses what the master provides.*	*The servants have their needs met.*

Who does the oikonomos serve? (Check one box)

☐ **He serves only the master.**

☐ **He serves only the household servants.**

☐ **He serves both the master and the servants.**

Did you check the third box? It is the correct one. The significance of the *oikonomos* is in serving as the middle man. He must *receive* before he can *give*! In the Kingdom of God, we serve knowing that the only resources we have are those provided by the Master. He gives to us that we may give to others. There is a great responsibility in serving as a *PAIS*, a servant of God.

A Christian must be sensitive to those who need rations. The Scripture says the food allowance must be given *at the proper time*. This requires a close relationship with those who are to receive the rations. The *oikonomos* doesn't sit in an office and dispense the food by remote control. He must know how much each person needs and the proper time for it to be provided. A relationship with those to *be served* is just as important as time spent with the Master to receive the resources from Him.

> 🌹 **Read 1 Corinthians 4:1-2. It describes the way the *oikonomos* is to be regarded by those being served. To help you grasp this truth, rewrite the two verses in your own words. Share your paraphrase with your mentor at your next get-together.**
>
> **v. 1:** _____
>
> _____
>
> _____
>
> **v. 2:** _____
>
> _____
>
> _____

The *oikonomos* must prove to be faithful in two directions: to the Master, and to those people she/he serves. This perfectly describes our life in the Kingdom. We must continually receive the "secret things of God." We are channels of His grace.

There is a third Scripture which uses the word *oikonomos*. It explains the "proper rations" to be distributed. 1 Peter 4:10 tells us, *"Each one should use whatever gift he has received to serve others, faithfully administering (oikonomos) God's grace in its various forms."*

The word for "gift" used by Peter refers to *spiritual capacities* given to us by the Holy Spirit. What we administer is a supernatural work of God flowing through us. There is much more involved than just providing food or clothing or shoes or money to people, although these may be included in our ministries. The "food" we are to give comes from God, not the ground. (That's what Jesus meant when he said to His disciples in John 4:32, *"I have food to eat that you know nothing about."*)

Serving as an *oikonomos* in the Kingdom requires us to recognize that the assets we "own" (money, property, etc.) actually belong to our Master. These tangibles have been entrusted to us for "proper distribution." Scripture makes it plain that a tithe of all we earn is to go *directly* to His ministry. Malachi 3:8 bluntly tells us if we do not do this, *we are thieves*!

The Chinese tell a story about a bamboo tree that stood tall above all the other plants in a beautiful garden. It proudly waved to those who passed by, proud to be the highest plant of all. One day the owner came and said, "Bamboo, I have need of you." Said the tree, "I know, master. I will gladly beckon people to visit your garden as I wave my branches high above all the other plants!" The master replied sadly, "No. You do not understand. The plants are dying for lack of water. I must cut you off at the roots, and then cut out your inner cavities. I will lay you on your side with one end placed in the river, so that water can flow through you to keep the plants alive. *I have need of you.*" Are you prepared for God to use you like that bamboo? *God has need of you!*

Week 4, Day 5
This Unit: The Kingdoms of This World
This Week: What's New?
Today: "Oikodomeo"

Read Romans 15:2; 1 Corinthians 14:26

🗝 **Match the Greek words below with their definitions by drawing
lines to connect them:**

PAIS   **Means "household"**

OIKOS   **Means "child" or "servant"**

OIKONOMOS   **Means "manager" or "steward"**

There is one more new word to consider: *oikodomeo*. It is also a member of the
oikos family tree, a first cousin of *oikonomos*.

The word is translated "build up" in many Scriptures. Some of these refer to the
construction of a building. A carpenter causes a structure to be *oikodomeo, built up*.

Other passages, including the two Scriptures listed above, use the word to describe
edifying, or *building up*, fellow Christians. It introduces us to a new understanding of
what it means to serve the Master by *building up* other persons.

Romans 15:2 uses the term: *"Each of us should please his neighbor for his good,
to build him up (oikodomeo)."* In His Kingdom, God desires to build you up through
your fellow cell group members.

As a young Christian, no one told me this. I was told to go into my "secret room"
and have a "quiet time" with the Lord. Just me and God — nobody else. I am glad
someone talked to me about being alone with God. It has become a lifelong habit, and
I strongly recommend it.

But no one told me about God coming to me through another believer to *oikodomeo*
me, to *build me up*. When I went away to college, I got away from the Lord and began to
live in a way that disgraced my Lord. One day, from the stress of living wrongly, I passed
out on the steps of the dormitory. An older student took me to his room and put me on
his bed. He spoke frankly to me. It was a major turning point in my life!

It was the first time I can remember someone in the Lord's family building me up.
He *oikodomeo, built me up*, not just by the words he spoke but by the presence of
Christ in him. The Master flowed into my spirit to cleanse, to correct, and to
encourage.

There is much loneliness among the people of God. We have broken persons who
need to be built up, to be restored to wholeness. It cannot be done individually. Christ
has indwelled others to come to me through them. My healing requires a pair of hands
to touch my pain!

One of the main purposes of a cell group church is to *oikodomeo* its members. It
requires small groups of persons who spend enough time together to love and trust
each other. If each person is an *oikonomos*, in touch with God, then the cell group
will *oikodomeo*.

🐟 **From 1 Corinthians 14:26, list five ways we can build up one another:**

1._____

2._____

3._____

4._____

5._____

🐟 **According to this verse, when the cell group gathers, how many are to become edifiers?**
(Check proper box or boxes)

☐   A few really spiritual members.

☐   Every person present.

☐   Only those who have no sins to confess.

☐   All of the above.

☐   None of the above.

If you checked the second box, you are correct! The Greek word translated "each of us" is very precise. It means that every person in the room — without exception — should share in building up, or edifying, the rest. This is one of your primary tasks as a citizen of the Kingdom — building up, and being built up, by the members of your cell group. Christ will empower you for this!

Week 5, Day 1
This Unit: The Servant Life
This Week: Equipped for Service
Today: Being Filled With the Spirit, Part 1

Read Galatians 5:16-21; John 7:37-39

Have you already experienced ups and downs in your life as a Christian? Have you been shocked to discover that many of your old habits and attitudes still plague you? Are you disgusted because of the *mess* in your life?

Perhaps you have already heard a voice whisper in your ear, "You can't make it in this Kingdom! This isn't for you!" If so, you are hearing *the voice of Satan*. He would be delighted to see you become discouraged with your new life.

There is *another* voice you are hearing. It's a voice that says, "You don't have to live on a roller coaster. There is a solution to your problem!"

 Read Galatians 5:16-21. Which ones of the "acts of the sinful nature" apply directly to you? (No need to write anything: just think about it!)

Think about the way these actions make you feel. Would you like to be set free from them? Would you like to have more of the fruit of the Spirit in your life (see Gal. 5:22-23)?

When you prayed to receive the Lord Jesus Christ as your Savior and Lord, you received His Holy Spirit, who resides *all the time* in your life. Scripture says there are four ways you can respond to His presence. Let's look at them:

1. You can *resist* the Spirit. In Acts 7:51, we read about people who went through religious rites, but who had no sensitivity to the leadership of the Holy Spirit. Whenever we clearly hear His voice speaking to us and we refuse to listen, we resist Him.
2. You can *grieve* the Spirit. In Ephesians 4:30-32, if we have bitterness, rage and anger, brawling and slander, or spitefulness and ill will, we grieve the Holy Spirit.
3. You can *quench* the Spirit. In 1 Thessalonians 5:19, we can "put out the Spirit's fire." It is a sad event when He ceases to burn within our hearts.
4. You can *be filled* with the Spirit. In Ephesians 5:18, the term for "be filled with the Spirit" is a *continuous verb*. Paul is saying, "be filled — and be filled — and *be filled* with the Spirit."

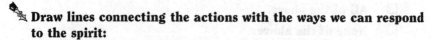 **Draw lines connecting the actions with the ways we can respond to the spirit:**

FILLED	**Refusing to heed His guidance.**
GRIEVE	**Going through forms of worship knowing you are rejecting the authority of the Holy Spirit.**
RESIST	**Longing for Christ's life to take control of every part of you.**
QUENCH	**Being nasty to a family member.**

HOW TO BE FILLED WITH THE SPIRIT

It is important for you to know that while the filling of the Holy Spirit is to be a constant flow of His life into yours, there is an experience in the Kingdom so powerful and dramatic that it begins a new relationship with God. People describe this experience in many ways. The different words used to describe the experience may be a bit confusing to you. It isn't important to settle on a single word or phrase to describe it, but the reality of it is not open to debate. All God has *given* me, He provided at the cross. But that doesn't mean I have *fully received* it.

There is a time in each of our lives when we say, "All I know about myself I give to all I know about You, Lord Jesus. Come in all of your power and take possession of all that I am."

In Genesis 32:26, Jacob came to that place. He had been a deceiver all his life. He had a history of cheating people. One night he came to the end of his self-respect. He wrestled with the Angel of God, saying, *"I will not let you go unless you bless me."* Everything about his life was changed as God touched him. It was such a change that God gave him a new name: "Israel."

Do you think the normal Christian life is a life of defeat? If so, realize that you are walking in your own strength and that you will fail. Will you let the Holy Spirit take control of your life now? Simply give up all self-effort to stop sinning. The Holy Spirit brings Christ-like character in your life. It is His "fruit" (Galatians 5:22-23). *He causes it*. Note that this passage does not refer to the *fruits* of the Spirit; they are the *fruit*. The Holy Spirit causes all these characteristics. Not just some of them, but *all of them*, will appear in every one in whom the Holy Spirit is given full control.

In John 4:14, we read the words of Jesus: *"but whoever drinks the water I give him will never thirst. Indeed, the water I give him will become in him a spring of water welling up to eternal life."*

According to John 7:37-39, who is symbolized by the "water" in John 4:14?

The H_____ S_____

A continual process for the Holy Spirit to control your life:

COME HUMBLY
"If a man is thirsty, let him come to me and drink." If that describes you, confess it to the Holy Spirit! Being filled begins by confessing you know you are not filled, and that you desire it with all your heart. Be humble!

ASK CONFIDENTLY
Jesus said, "And I will do whatever you ask in my name, so that Son may bring glory to the Father." Jesus told his believers to hold nothing back in their requests. Be bold in your requests!

RECEIVE THANKFULLY
You may experience the Holy Spirit like waves of power and joy or like a gentle calm. Regardless of the way He comes, He comes with power! The Spirit's presence in your life is a gift. Be thankful!

Week 5, Day 2
This Unit: The Servant Life
This Week: Equipped for Service
Today: Being Filled With the Spirit, Part 2

Read Luke 11:11-13; Acts 9:17

A teacher in a science class asked a student to fill an eight-ounce glass with water. The teacher then poured four ounces of sand into the glass. Of course, half of the water ran over the sides and was lost. The teacher demonstrated *the law of displacement*. That is, two substances cannot occupy the same space at the same time.

When we ask to be filled with the Spirit, we must first examine ourselves. If the substances of disobedience and unbelief fill our minds and hearts, there is little space left for His Spirit to reign. Thus, being *filled* means there must also be an *emptying*. If we have a cynical spirit, there is no room for faith. If we have a bitterness in our soul, there is no room for joy. When our "inner man" is empty, there is plenty of room for the Holy Spirit to fill us with His own presence.

Thousands of believers live in the Kingdom of God without being filled with the Spirit. (Have you already met your share of them?) There is a simple reason for this. They have dug in their "spiritual heels" and have said, "This is as far as I feel comfortable going in the Kingdom of God. I will *never* be overly zealous. I must always be in control!" Often they will settle on doctrinal positions to justify their unwillingness to be totally emptied of self. They are never immersed into the deep things of God!

When you are totally lost in the presence of the Spirit of God, you can look and feel foolish. I have seen strong men sob uncontrollably in public when the Lord touched them. If you need to protect your "dignity" at all costs, the filling of the Spirit may frighten you.

Dion Robert pastors a huge cell group church in the Ivory Coast. He tells of a night when he was reading Ezekiel 47 and came to the passage where the prophet was led into water that was ankle-deep. He was further led into knee-deep water, then waist-deep water, and then into a current over his head, "a river that no one could cross" (Ezekiel 47:5). Pastor Dion said that night the Lord spoke to him and asked, "Dion, are you prepared for Me to lead you into a river so deep and so swift, that your feet will no longer touch the bottom? Will you follow Me into the deep things of the Kingdom and let Me fully use you as My servant?" He struggled with the call of God then cried out, "Yes! Yes! Yes!" It was from that night that the Lord put Dion Robert's hands around West Africa, and then Europe, and even the United States, and used him to draw thousands and thousands of people into the Kingdom of God.

Why do you desire to be filled with the Spirit? If you cry to the Lord with a wrong motive, He will not fill you. If your motive is to boast or gloat and get attention by receiving great power from God, you need to confess that as sin — as "sand in the glass" of your soul. But when you desire to become a more effective *PAIS* for the Lord, to be a better instrument of God, to show forth a Christ-like spirit, you may be certain God will honor your request to be filled. When you are filled with the Spirit, your life will be turned upside down! Many things that you now consider important will lose their attraction.

Most important of all, you will move into the deeper portions of the Kingdom and discover treasures you never expected to find. I would like to share with you that there have been moments in my own life when the presence of the Lord became so precious and so strong that I did not think I could catch my next breath!

🌹 **Read Luke 11:11-13. What is the Father's reaction when you ask Him for the Holy Spirit? (As you meditate on these verses, write below the thoughts God gives you.**

_____

_____

_____

_____

If you are a person who brought deep hurts into the Kingdom as part of your baggage, you may maintain a dark isolation from other people. Here is a special word for you. Often when this has happened, we are afraid to trust anyone again — the pain is so intense! Yet, your inner being cries out for healing. How will the Spirit minister to you? You will find your answer in your cell group family! It may happen as you share with one person, or with the group. Because God knows you need support, the filling of the Holy Spirit for you may involve others.

🌹 **Read Acts 9:17: what did Ananias do with his hands to bring sight and the Holy Spirit to Paul?**

He P_____ his hands O_____ S_____.

Ananias said, "the Lord . . . has sent me so that you may see again and be filled with the Holy Spirit." Ananias obeyed the Lord, placed his hands upon him, and let God's Spirit flow through him to minister to the blinded man.

Many times in Scripture, God sends His Spirit through another person's touch. That is the reason why you are attached to a cell group, a "Basic Christian Community." Each one of us can become the agent of God's love and grace to our brothers and sisters in the Kingdom. Saul needed Ananias. The eunuch needed Philip. Cornelius needed Peter. In each case, the Holy Spirit sent these people as agents of God's grace. In fact, the book of Acts is filled with similar examples of the way God works *through* one person to meet the needs of *another* person.

🌹 **Review: draw lines to connect the words below to their definitions: (If you need help, refer to pages 40, 44, 46, and 48.)**

PAIS	Means "build up" or "edify"
OIKOS	Means "child" or "servant"
OIKONOMOS	Means "household"
OIKODOMEO	Means "manager" or "steward"

Week 5, Day 3
This Unit: The Servant Life
This Week: Equipped for Service
Today: The Spirit's Energizings, Part 1

Read 1 Corinthians 12:1-11

We should desire to be filled with the Holy Spirit so that we can minister to others as His power flows through us. These supernatural activities are called "gifts." In the original text, there are several words used to describe this work of the Spirit. Verse 1 speaks of them as the "supernaturals," or "breathings." They are then called "grace gifts" in verse 4, and in verse 6 and elsewhere, "energizings."

These spiritual energies are the movement of the Holy Spirit. They do not exist apart from Him. They are not available to unbelievers. Also, the Christian does not decide when and where they will be exercised. We do not use the gifts of the Holy Spirit. Instead, He fills us and flows His power through us according to His own will, time, and place.

1 Corinthians 12:7 tells us, *"Now to each one the manifestation [demonstration] of the Spirit is given for the common good."* The work of the Holy Spirit is to take place not only *in* us, but also *through* us. The gifts are used for the benefit and growth of the body of Christ. That is why your cell group places a major emphasis on each person being available to "build up" *(oikodomeo)* others as the gifts manifest.

How do you receive the gifts? Look at verse 7 again. Paul says they are given *"to each one"*! That little phrase is very clear: it includes *you!* The Holy Spirit does not select a "special group." If you walk in the fullness of the Holy Spirit, then the Holy Spirit will use you to impart the gifts to others.

Therefore, it is more correct to say that we are all *distributors* of the gifts, rather than the receivers of them. Verse 11 says, *"All these are the work of one and the same Spirit, and he gives them to each one, just as he determines."*

Don't be anxious about whether the Spirit will give you a certain gift. It's not necessary to repeatedly pray for God to work through you. Relax! Enjoy your fellowship with Him! Your availability and fellowship with Him will cause ministry to flow through you. Gradually, you will discover something about the way God uses you. It will be appropriate to your personality.

I remember a middle-aged woman named Ellie. She was a quiet woman who didn't attract a lot of attention to herself. No one would have called her "super spiritual." She just quietly loved her Lord and faithfully walked in His Spirit. As a pastor, I would be called to homes where a death had occurred. Usually by the time I arrived, Ellie had somehow heard about it and was already there. As I comforted the grieving family, she was in the kitchen, washing dishes and fixing coffee. She would quietly change all the beds and do the laundry in anticipation of the coming of relatives who would be spending the night there.

What she did was more than being a "good neighbor." I could sense the real presence of the Holy Spirit in her, empowering her to exercise the lovely spiritual gift of being "able to help others" (1 Corinthians 12:28).

Years later, when I was no longer pastoring, I received an emergency call from a crisis "hot line:" "Dr. Neighbour, we have just had a phone call from a house near you. The wife was sick with the flu, and her husband stood at the foot of the bed and blew his brains out. She and the children are hysterical. Please go right over."

After the body had been removed and the wife and children had been taken to the house next door, I looked at the blood on the rug and the bedclothes. I knew this horrific scene could not be left for that dear family to see! Who could I call for help? Of course! Ellie! Quickly, I picked up the phone and dialed her. She came immediately, with bottles of seltzer water and rags. Together, we knelt and scrubbed until we removed all traces of the tragedy.

Like Dorcas (Acts 9:36-41), Ellie manifested the gift of *helping others in distress*. It is proper that her gift did not demonstrate her "spirituality" but was used to edify others.

As you discover the Holy Spirit empowering you for ministry, search the Scriptures and study the times when others used those gifts. Meditate on the way you were used to bless another person, and thank your Lord for the privilege of being His *PAIS*.

Carefully read 1 Corinthians 12:1-11. Find the verses where these thoughts are found. Write proper references in the left column:

_____ The Holy Spirit enables us to say, "Jesus is Lord."

_____ Messages of wisdom and knowledge are gifts.

_____ Faith and gifts of healing are gifts.

_____ Our gifts are given for the common good.

_____ The Holy Spirit decides who gets what gift.

_____ This verse mentions God and workings.

_____ This verse mentions the Lord and service.

_____ This verse mentions the Spirit and gifts.

_____ Do not be ignorant about spiritual gifts.

_____ We used to believe power came from ido

Week 5, Day 4
This Unit: The Servant Life
This Week: Equipped for Service
Today: The Spirit's Energizing, Part 2

Read 1 Corinthians 12:31-14:1

When I lived in Singapore, I could look outside the window of my apartment and see a canal. I often looked down on that canal, and from the fourth floor, I noticed how carefully it was constructed. Slabs of concrete gave it a solid base and sides, and there were ports to cause rainwater to flow into it. When the weather was dry, the canal was totally empty. But when the heavy rains fell, the canal filled to the brim with a rushing current of water.

The great value of the canal was not seen when the sun was shining. Only when it rained did those of us who lived nearby appreciate it. If the canal did not exist, the entire area would be a massive mud hole!

Think of the gifts of the Holy Spirit as "spiritual slabs of concrete" God uses to allow *the current of love* to flow from Him, through us, to others. Paul explains in this chapter that if we try to separate our understanding of spiritual gifts from their purpose, they are totally worthless. Therefore, the focus should be on the *activity* of the gifts, not their possession.

1 Corinthians 14:1 tells us to *"Follow the way of love and eagerly desire spiritual gifts . . ."* This truth gives us a powerful basis to evaluate the source of spiritual gifts. Sometimes they are used in a situation where people are awestruck by their presence, and the person manifesting them is seen as a "super-Christian." One way to evaluate the use of a gift is the motive which produces it. If that motive is *love*, we may be sure it comes from above. If not, its source is to be questioned. In fact, 1 Corinthians 14:29 tells us to "weigh carefully what is said." Paul's extensive teaching in Chapter 13 makes it plain that the gifts should flow from love and if love is not present, something is out of order.

The word for *"love"* used in this passage in the original language is *agape*. Are you familiar with it? There are three Greek words translated "love." The first one is *phileo*, meaning "brotherly love." The second one is *eros*, referring to a love used for self-gratification. *Agape* is radically different. It speaks of a love that comes from the character of the one doing the loving, not from the beauty of the person receiving the love.

Notice this third usage in Romans 5:8: "But God demonstrates his own love *(agape)* for us in this: While we were still sinners, Christ died for us." There was certainly nothing attractive about us when we were sinners! Yet, His love overlooked our ugliness and He gave His life for us.

In your cell group, there may be people with unappealing problems. Your first reaction may be, "Oh, dear — I want to leave this person alone!" At that instant, you may be sure there are *two problems* in the group, and *you* are the second one. If there is no love, there will be no need for the gifts to be manifested through you. The first requirement of being a channel for the grace gifts is to have *agape* love.

🦅 **What would you do?**
Each of the situations described below actually took place in a cell group:

1. **Susan bought thousands of dollars of clothes and trinkets using her credit cards. Unable to pay the bills, she ran from the community. She finally shares her secret with your cell group. What would you do? (There are no "right" answers.)**

☐   Offer to loan her money to pay the debt
☐   Tell her to get two jobs to pay off the debt
☐   Remain silent. She made the mess — let her clean it up!
☐   ? _____

2. **A couple in your cell group have a 17-year-old daughter who stayed out all night with her boyfriend. They are filled with anxiety! They ask you to counsel them. What would you do?**

☐   Pray for God to help them and withdraw
☐   Talk to the daughter alone on their behalf
☐   ? _____

3. **A cell member's child has bruises on his face. It is obvious the father is responsible. In the cell, he claims to have a "gift of prophecy," and is often arrogant. What would you do?**

☐   Strongly rebuke him as a hypocrite.
☐   Seek to understand his spiritual bankruptcy.
☐   ? _____

In each of these cases, the people were demonstrating an inner spiritual problem that could not be solved without help. None of them could "break through" to God alone. All of them were prisoners of wrong values.

Do you recognize how *agape* love will have to operate in these situations? The flow of spiritual gifts is desperately needed. The gifts of wise speech, helping others in distress, discerning true and false spirits — these and others are needed. The Holy Spirit is the Source of their solution, and He uses us as the *agents* to help those who are powerless to deal with their problems alone.

It is a costly thing to show *agape* to another person who may not be attractive to us because of his or her situation. "Messy" is a good word to describe their lives! Sometimes spiritual gifts provide guidance or support. These people may require the *agents* (that's us!) to enter the mess for a period of time, not just for a cell group session. As God's love fills your heart, you will be used!

Week 5, Day 5
This Unit: The Servant Life
This Week: Equipped for Service
Today: The Spirit's Energizings, Part 3

Read 1 Corinthians 14:1, 3, 5, 12, 24-26

In this chapter, Paul sought to correct an early problem in church life. People were gathering in their home groups without exhibiting the *agape* love we learned about yesterday. In chapter 11:20-30, he speaks of their lack of concern for one another, and says that many are spiritually sick as a result. If the gifts are not used to build up *(oikodomeo)* one another, they will be abused.

If you have time after reading today's materials, read 1 Cor. 14 in its entirety. Keep this thought in your mind: *These Christians were exercising spiritual gifts without agape!* That is the whole point of the chapter.

Think about the gifts we have discussed. How many of them can be exercised *without regard for their ministry to others?* Healing? Helping others in distress? Discerning true and false spirits? All involve *agape* ministry to others. We must recognize that *all* of the gifts are to involve the believer in ministry! The church did not understand this.

> **According to verses 1, 5, 12, and 24-26, which spiritual gift is highly useful?**
>
> ☐   **Healing**
> ☐   **Prophecy**
> ☐   **Speaking in tongues**

If you checked "prophecy," you are correct. What is this gift? How is it exercised? A study of the Old Testament reveals that the Hebrew word for "prophet" is literally, "mouthpiece." God came upon the prophet, and he spoke divinely given words. Often these were predictions of events far in the future. It was through the gift of prophecy that the Bible was written for us (see 2 Peter 1:21). While a prophecy today may still foretell future events, it has a broader purpose. Examine carefully the teaching in 1 Corinthians 14:3: *"But everyone who prophesies speaks to men for their strengthening, encouragement and comfort."* Then in verse 26, we are told everyone should have *"a hymn, or a word of instruction, a revelation, a tongue or an interpretation."* Thus, the word "prophecy" can be seen as a *general term* describing gifts that strengthen, encourage, and comfort. It can also describe a *distinct gift* — prophecy.

It would seem that Paul has both meanings in mind in this chapter. The one fact we may be certain of is that any use of spiritual gifts not accompanied by *agape* flowing freely, is an abuse and a misuse of them.

🐟 **In 1 Corinthians 14:26, how many people in a gathering of believers are to flow with spiritual gifts?**

- ☐ A few who are "tuned in" to the Lord.
- ☐ The people who pray a lot.
- ☐ Everyone — every single person present!
- ☐ Don't know for sure.

It is vital for you to know how many people in a gathering of believers are expected to exercise spiritual gifts. As you think about it, the first thing to consider is: *how many people were involved in this "coming together?"* Did Paul see 120 people in the gathering, or 1,000, or a larger gathering? I believe he was speaking of *house groups*, cell groups, and not a large assembly of people.

The second fact to know is that the original language uses a precise word for "everyone" in verse 26. It means *every single person, with no exceptions, is to manifest spiritual gifts for the edification of others.* Thus, he says our calling as *PAIS* people is to freely show love *(agape)* to one another and to become channels of God's grace for our cell group.

ONE COIN, TWO SIDES: PAIS - CHILD/SERVANT

🐟 **In 1 Corinthians 14:24-25, what happens when an unbeliever or someone who does not understand sees the ministry of the gifts flowing in your group?**

"He will be C_____ by A_____ that he

is a sinner and will be judged by A_____, and

the S_____ of his heart will be laid bare."

Were you again impressed by the words *"by all"* used twice in this passage? *"Each one . . . by all . . ."* makes it plain that God intends to use every one of us, without exception, to bless others.

You are part of this "all." If you wait for the "real ministers" to do the ministry, someone could miss his opportunity to meet God. God wants to move through you to minister to others. You might think that this is beyond your abilities. You are right. Don't look at your talents, at what you cannot do. You don't have to be a great preacher or sing like an angel. He only wants you to listen to Him and share what He gives you with others.

While there are hours and hours of study about this whole area in the Kingdom for you, these are very basic truths to help you as you journey onward. Go now to the "Listening Room" and pray for each person in your cell group. Ask the Lord for a special scripture that you can share in the next meeting.

Week 6, Day 1
This Unit: The Servant Life
This Week: Touching God
Today: "The Listening Room"

Read Galatians 2:20; Romans 7:22; 1 Thessalonians 5:23

A Japanese pastor invited an American pastor to visit his home. The Japanese pastor took his guest to a lovely garden behind the house, where a one-room cottage stood. The pastor explained: "This is my *'listening room.'*"

In the Kingdom of God, you need a "Listening Room." A *PAIS* ministers only *after* he/she receives the Master's orders. Hearing the directions of God for our own needs, the needs of others, and for His assignments to us should have top priority. Praying is more than a one-way conversation in which you speak to God; it also involves *listening* to Him.

There are four questions we need to consider this week about our life in the Kingdom of God. The first is, *"Where is God when I commune with Him?"* Do you think of Him as "seated above the circle of the heavens," listening to you from outer space? Do you always look toward the ceiling or the stars when you pray? If so, that long distance may cause Him to seem very remote to you.

Galatians 2:20 tells us, *". . . Christ lives in me."* The presence of God should not be considered to be "out there," but "in here." The fellowship we have with the Father is very intimate. He is a friend who sticks *closer than a brother* (Proverbs 18:24).

Wherever you go, He is there with you, and He speaks with you. You may be sure of that! In Moses' day, men never came into *direct* contact with God. They only knew of His presence in their midst by a cloud of smoke or fire. That is not true for us. God desires us to respond to His presence within us and live our whole life with Him. This is to be known to us in conscious experience.

The second question we need to consider is, *"Which part of me communes with God?"* In Romans 7:22 we read, *"For in my inner being I delight in God's law."* Resident within your inner being *(see diagram on page 61)* lives the Triune God — Father, Son, and Holy Spirit. When you pray, you are communing with your Lord and your Master. Therefore, your fellowship with Him takes place as you yield to your King and declare that you are part of His Kingdom.

> In 1 Thessalonians 5:23, where does Paul say he desires us to be sanctified ("set apart, made holy")?
>
> S_____ T, S_____L, and B_____Y

> Who does he ask to do this to us?
>
> The G_____ of P_____E

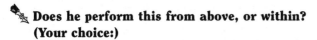**Does he perform this from above, or within? (Your choice:)**

☐ **Above**

☐ **Within**

Ephesians 3:20 tells us our God *"is able to do immeasurably more than all we ask or imagine, according to his power that is at work within us, . . ."*

Our "Listening Room" is more an attitude, a value of our lives, than a special room built for that purpose. It is a condition in which we not only *speak* to Him, but also *hear* from Him. God does speak! The problem comes when we do not know how to *listen* to His voice. To obtain peace of mind, and His direction for our steps and our ministry to others through use of our spiritual gifts, we need to hear Him when He speaks. There is no more important location in the Kingdom of God than the "Listening Room"!

Dr. A. W. Tozer wrote in *The Pursuit of God,*

The highest love of God is not intellectual, it is spiritual. God is spirit and only the spirit of man can know Him really. In the deep spirit of a man the fire must glow or his love is not the true love of God . . . Men of the breaking hearts had a quality about them not known to nor understood by common men. (pp. 40-43)

During the days ahead, we will refer again to this diagram. Are you curious about the "strongholds"? Those represent old baggage we brought with us when we arrived in the Kingdom. They don't belong in our lives. God is working in us to remove them. As you learn to yield and listen to His voice, He will tell you what to do about the strongholds.

In 1 Samuel 3:8, Samuel heard a voice calling and did not know the source. As he continued to listen, he discovered that *God was the caller*. We need never fear that God will quit speaking to us. If we miss His message the first time, He will continue to speak until He gets our attention!

Now, close this book and *listen* to His voice. Be silent for the next little while. Say, "Lord I am listening!" From the depths of your spirit, He will speak. Worship Him as He does so, and know that in your deepest spirit God may remove a stronghold or offer a word of guidance. *LISTEN!*

Week 6, Day 2
This Unit: The Servant Life
This Week: Touching God
Today: How to Hear God's Voice, Part 1

Read Luke 5:16; 6:12; 21:37; 22:39-46

The four Scriptures above speak of an important habit in the life of our Lord. In Luke 6:12, He was at the beginning of His ministry. He had a major decision to make. The Son of God was about to assemble His "cell group." *(It is important to note that even our Lord performed His ministry with close ties to twelve men — and all of them had "warts and pimples"!)* Before He made that choice, He spent an entire night in the "Listening Room." The decision was made only after He had heard from the Father and the Holy Spirit.

In Luke 21:37, Jesus was at the end of His ministry. He was busy throughout the day teaching, but at night He retired to His "Listening Room" on the Mount of Olives. This was His custom.

In Luke 22:39-46, once again we see Him praying into the night. The agony of the Cross had already begun for Him. At Calvary, His *body* would be crucified, but it was in the "Listening Room" that His *will* was crucified as He said, "Father, if you are willing, take this cup from me; yet not my will, but yours be done." The intensity of His prayer caused Him to sweat great drops of blood, an indication of extreme inner agony.

There were other occasions when He went away to be with the Father, including 40 days and nights in the wilderness after His baptism. In Matthew 14:23, we find Him alone in a remote mountainside "Listening Room." On another mountain peak, far to the north of Capernaum, He was transfigured while praying (Luke 9:28-35).

Since the Son of God had a "Listening Room," we need one, too! Every major and minor event of our lives in the Kingdom will require time to hear the words of the Master.

> **Currently, how much of your day do you spend in the "Listening Room"? (You can include the time you spend in this booklet but not as a substitute for listening to his voice.)**
>
> ☐ No time at all.
> ☐ Once in a while, but not regularly.
> ☐ Less than an hour a day.
> ☐ An hour a day or more.

Do you realize our lives are ordered by what we *value the most*? From time to time through the years I have tried to take up playing golf and have given it up each time. The reason? Knocking a white ball around for several hours is boring to me. Ruthie loves to watch a baseball game, but I take along a book to read. Give me a quiet room and a computer to write books, and I am very happy. *We are guided by our value systems in all we do.* If we do not value time spent in the "Listening Room," we will make endless excuses to explain away the need for it. Thus, we live unguided lives. Think of the folly of wandering around, year after year, following your nose without any sense of direction from the King of kings! Does it make sense to you?

> ✍ **Use the space below to talk to yourself about this. If you choose, show what you have written to your mentor, or share it with your cell group at the next meeting.**

_____

_____

How does God's Spirit speak to me? As you learn to hear Him, He will speak to *your mind* by giving an idea, or an understanding of a situation. He may speak to *your will* by calling you to do what He deems best. He may speak to *your spirit*, by giving peace when you are troubled — or making you feel troubled when you are at peace. He may speak through *your memory*, to help you recall His help in the past. Or, He may speak to *your heart* by reminding you that you are breaking God's spiritual laws, and you feel lousy.

You may be certain of one thing: *If you will take time to be with Him, you will certainly hear His voice.* Solomon wrote, *"he taught me and said, 'Lay hold of my words with all your heart; keep my commands and you will live . . .'"* (Proverbs 4:4). Making time to be alone to listen to His words will require a re-sorting of your values. There's a basic law of economics that says, "If you spend money to purchase 'A,' you won't have it to buy 'B'!" Perhaps more important than how you spend your money is how you spend your time. Think about it.

> ✍ **How much time do you presently devote to each activity, and what will you revise to have time for your "Listening Room" experience?**

ACTIVITY	TIME SPENT DAILY/WEEKLY
"Listening Room"	_____
Recreation	_____
Work/school	_____
Watching television	_____
Shopping	_____
Cell group life	_____
Doing nothing	_____
Talking to friends	_____
Being with family	_____
Reading, studying	_____

Week 6, Day 3
This Unit: The Servant Life
This Week: Touching God
Today: How to Hear God's Voice, Part 2

Read 1 Peter 1:10-12, 16-20; Matthew 22:29

What is the relationship between Scripture and your time in the "Listening Room"? First of all, let's discover the One who caused the Scriptures to be written. In 1 Peter 1:10-11 we read, *"the prophets . . . searched intently and with the greatest care, trying to find out the time and circumstances to which the Spirit of Christ in them was pointing . . ."*

Underline the above verses in your Bible! Jesus Christ, Who dwells in you, also dwelled in the writers of Scripture and caused them to record their words. The Scripture says *"It was revealed to them that they were not serving themselves but you . . . ."* Scriptures have a very important place in your life, and should always be included in your "Listening Room" time.

Since Christ is the Author of Scripture, you may be certain that the word He speaks directly to you never violates His Scripture. There will be a continual relationship between what you read in your Bible and what you hear as you listen to the voice of the Holy Spirit. Scripture must always confirm the voice of God. Christ will never, ever contradict the Scripture with a different word to you. Here are some passages for you to think about. Ponder over each one, perhaps underlining them in your Bible:

Romans 15:4: *"For everything that was written in the past was written to teach us, so that through endurance and the encouragement of the Scriptures we might have hope."*

2 Timothy 3:15: *"and how from infancy you have known the holy Scriptures, which are able to make you wise for salvation through faith in Christ Jesus."*

Luke 24:27: *"And beginning with Moses and all the Prophets, he explained to them what was said in all the Scriptures concerning himself."*

Luke 24:32: *"They asked each other, 'Were not our hearts burning within us while he talked with us on the road and opened the Scriptures to us?'"*

John 10:35: *". . . the Scripture cannot be broken . . ."*

We must always have the Bible with us in the "Listening Room." Any thought which is not appropriate to the Bible's teaching should be instantly rejected.

In this illustration, the inspired truth of Scripture is received by the mind, as it is read and understood. There is a special word to describe what happens next: *illumination.* As I direct my heart and mind together to seek the Lord, His Spirit speaks into my heart, directly impressing His thoughts and ideas upon me. At such times, I will experience the presence of God in a powerful way. You may find yourself in deep worship, in praise, in searching confession of sin, or in sensing a call to do a special ministry for Him. God will give you answers to problems and heartaches. God may lead you to speak to someone about his/her need for Christ. The Father may give you an encouraging word for someone in your cell group or your family.

The times Jesus spent in fellowship with the Father were not ritualistic formalities. He craved the communion such hours provided to Him. It will be the same for you! In the Kingdom of God, our fellowship with the Lord and with others in His body is an exclusive privilege never comprehended by unbelievers!

🌿 **In Matthew 22:29, Jesus told the Sadducees (who did not believe in the resurrection of the dead) they were in error for two reasons. What were they?**

They did not know the

_____

They did not know the

_____

of _____.

🌿 **Of the comments below, which ones do you agree with?**

☐ **Knowing scriptures alone is adequate.**

☐ **Knowing God's power alone is adequate.**

☐ **Both must be present in the "Listening Room."**

☐ **Illumination takes place when scriptures and God's power are present in the "Listening Room."**

Let's begin to experience "illumination" right now. Turn in your Bible to 2 Corinthians 3:17-18. Ask the Holy Spirit to come and teach you about this passage — not only what it means, but also what it means to you.

As you reflect on this passage, write down your thoughts. Discover the power of the scriptures, as well as the meaning, by praying over its message for you.

Week 6, Day 4
This Unit: The Servant Life
This Week: Touching God
Today: How to Hear God's Voice, Part 3

Read Romans 8:5-7; 8:27; 12:2

Thoughtfully read the Scriptures above in the order that they are given. All of them explain that our Teacher is the Holy Spirit, Who will guide us into "all truth." We have already established that whether He does that through a Scripture verse or by speaking directly to us, He will never contradict what Scripture teaches.

Bible meditation combines the analysis of the mind with the spontaneity of the heart. Living in the Kingdom of God does not mean throwing your mind away. You are to use both your mind and your spirit (the "inner man") as you approach God.

Before you submitted to God's reign over you, the powers of darkness had freedom to control your mind (Romans 8:7) and your spirit. That is no longer true! Your mind and spirit can now communicate with the Holy Spirit, who will guide you into truth.

✎ Rate where you are at this time:

TRUE	FALSE	
☐	☐	**Most of the time, true reality for me is in physical, not spiritual experiences.**
☐	☐	**Most of the time, my goal is to develop my mind rather than my spirit.**
☐	☐	**I live out of what my mind, not what my spirit tells me to do about situations.**
☐	☐	**I have calculated, analytical thoughts, rather than flowing thoughts placed in my mind by the spirit of God.**
☐	☐	**I focus more time on academic study of scripture than on spending time with the Lord in fellowship, worship, and communion.**
☐	☐	**I make decisions based on analysis of knowledge; I do not know how to quietly wait on the Lord until he spontaneously gives me His thoughts, His burdens, and His visions.**
☐	☐	**I seldom experience God speaking to me directly, guiding what I am to share or to do.**

WHAT MAKES GOD'S VOICE DIFFERENT?

1. You sense the thoughts are coming from your "inner being," not just your mind. This is not new to you! Each time you say, "I love you" to someone, the source is not your mind, is it?
2. The thoughts given by the Holy Spirit are often unprompted by your own ideas.
3. The thoughts are flowing, not the result of exerting yourself.
4. The thoughts will have a distinctive message.
5. You will sense the words you are receiving are different than your own.
6. You will sense God's presence, along with an awareness of His power.

Hebrews 5:14 tells us that by constant listening to the Spirit you will be trained *"to distinguish good from evil."* To repeat: *God speaks!* Until you begin to distinguish His voice from your own thoughts, you may simply group His words with your thoughts and not realize what He has said to you.

1 John 4:1 tells you, *"do not believe every spirit, but test the spirits to see whether they are from God, because many false prophets have gone out into the world."* If you are unsure of the source of your thoughts, ask yourself: "Does this thought glorify Jesus? Is it true to Scripture?"

The prophet Isaiah wrote, *"Then I heard the voice of the Lord saying, 'Whom shall I send? And who will go for us?' And I said, 'Here am I. Send me!'" (Isaiah 6:8)* You can fully expect your Lord to guide you, too, into ministry! Isaiah also wrote, *"Whether you turn to the right or to the left, your ears will hear a voice behind you, saying, 'This is the way; walk in it.'" (Isaiah 30:21)*

For centuries, men and women have chronicled accounts of their times in the "Listening Room." These writers preserved their journals because they were valuable to them. Some of the journals were so profound that they have been republished for generations.

I recommend that you create a personal "Listening Room" journal. In it, record the unprompted flow of thoughts that come to your mind. In the beginning, listening to God's voice will be strange. You may say to yourself, "Is that thought from God or from myself?" Such moments of pondering may hinder your fellowship with Him. Later, you can review what you have written to prayerfully discern whether the truths were given by the Lord.

A simple notebook is sufficient, or you may use a voice recorder, or a computer to journal what Spirit is saying to you. Many generations ago, John Wesley wrote all of his "Listening Room" journals in a secret code he devised, which took many years to decipher. As you bare your soul to the Lord, and He speaks to you, some of the things He says may be very personal. Therefore, this is not something you will share freely. Be sure to date each entry!

Athletes become proficient by constant practice and exercise. Some moves become automatic for them in a competition because they have done them over and over. It's much the same in the Kingdom of God. Practicing the presence of God is an exercise that will plunge you into deeper fellowship with him than you have ever known.

Why wait? Begin your journal today!

Week 6, Day 5
This Unit: The Servant Life
This Week: Touching God
Today: How to Hear God's Voice, Part 4

Read Luke 10:38-42; Romans 12:11

🔖 **Martha sought to provide food for her special guest. Mary had a stronger desire: she just wanted to be with Jesus. Ask yourself: if Jesus were to come to your house, would you probably act like Mary, or Martha?**

☐   **Martha**

☐   **Mary**

Our value systems cause us to react to the same situation in very different ways. Martha considered her *service* for Jesus to be the most important matter. Mary considered *being with* Jesus to be most important.

There have been periods in my life when I felt my *service* for the Lord was the most important thing I could do. In every case, I began to feel His power drain away from my ministry. With alarm, I would realize I had become like Martha. Like her, one of the marks of my condition was a critical spirit toward others who "didn't work as hard for the Lord as I did." That attitude caused the deep flow of *agape* love within me to be absent, and my spirit wounded those around me. At the end of those periods, my "Listening Room" had to become my confession booth! (1 John 1:9). You and I must always remember that God does not consider us to be significant *because of what we do*, but rather because of *who we are*! Whenever we do something *for* Him that stops us from being *with* Him, we are like Martha. It's possible to do both.

🔖 **In Luke 10:41-42, what did Jesus say when Martha complained to him about Mary? (Rewrite his answer in your own words.)**

_____

_____

_____

🔖 **In Luke 10:41-42, when Jesus said, "Mary has chosen what is better," what did he mean?**

☐   **Allowing practical things to replace spending time with the Lord is not recommended.**

☐   **Preparing food for guests is not important.**

☐   **Both of the above are correct.**

☐   **Neither of the above is correct.**

In Romans 12:11 Paul writes, *"Never be lacking in zeal, but keep your spiritual fervor, serving the Lord."* Another way of saying that might be, "Don't slow down what you are doing, but don't neglect time in the 'Listening Room.'"

It's just not possible to do the *work* of the Lord without His *power*. To become a channel of that power, we must be in constant contact with Him.

PRAYING — UNTIL!

Lydia M. Swain, personal assistant to pastor Yonggi Cho in Seoul, Korea, teaches the importance of *"praying — until!"* She told me of one occasion when the Lord gave her a deep burden for her daughter back in America. She was so overcome that she fasted and prayed for days. She only knew her daughter was, or would soon be, in grave danger. After a lengthy time of remaining in the "Listening Room" the Lord spoke: "It's all right now, Lydia. You can rest assured that I will care for her."

A short time later, her daughter called to recount what had happened to her. She was flying on a plane 30,000 feet in the air when she started to unfasten her seat belt to walk down the aisle. A powerful word from the Lord came to her: *"Do not unfasten your seat belt!"* Confused, she sat meditating about what she had heard in her spirit. Seconds later, a man got up and quickly rushed to the door of the plane. Throwing it open, he jumped to his death. *Everything that was not fastened down was sucked out of the open door!*

Mrs. Swain told me that through the years she has learned not just to pray, but to pray until a burden is lifted. Do not forget this important truth. Keep your spiritual fervor as you serve the Lord.

LISTENING FOR EDIFICATION TO OTHERS

Take seriously the assignment to *oikodomeo*, "to build up" others. In your cell group, you will learn of needs and problems in the lives of others. Take those needs to the "Listening Room." Hear what God says to you about the source of problems, their solutions, and how to share with others what He tells you.

I have often left a cell group meeting without a clear word from the Lord for a problem that surfaced in one of the group members. In the "Listening Room," God provides guidance for me — a word to be shared at the next meeting or through a private conversation. You can also experience this as you "pray through" needs within the lives of others.

When you sense the Lord is giving you a message that will minister to another person, write it in your "Listening Room" diary and meditate on it. He may also show you how to share it. There may be times when He gives you a special word about a physical problem in your own life or in the life of someone else. Do not pray for the sick simply to see something supernatural happen. Jesus healed because of His *compassion* for those who were suffering. Although He is not obligated to answer our prayers the way we may desire, *God does hear and answer our requests*.

For example, in my cell group, Nancy received word that her daughter-in-law was going to have a terribly malformed child. Several scans verified this fact, right up to the end of the pregnancy. Nancy went to her "Listening Room" and agonized in prayer over the child's condition. God heard her sobs, and His healing presence touched the fetus. *The child was perfectly normal at birth.* Nancy had "prayed until," and God had touched that unborn boy. By faith, trust Him to use you to also bring His perfect will to others!

Week 7, Day 1
This Unit: Personal, Please
This Week: Dealing with Strongholds
Today: Recognizing the Problem

Read Ephesians 4:17-24; Philippians 2:12; 1 Corinthians 10:13

🌹 **On page 17 (week 1, day 4), we learned a definition for a "stronghold." Can you select it from the list below without looking back? If not, reread that page.**

☐ **A stronghold describes an inner condition where Satan still has power to control.**

☐ **A stronghold is a fortified place where a power has control.**

☐ **Both of the above are correct**

Note the phrase "a *Christian* with an inner condition . . ." Only Christians can have strongholds. Unbelievers do not have them. They are *totally* controlled by Satan. Refer to the diagram on page 61, noting that strongholds can exist in the body and the soul (the mind, the will, and the emotions) of a believer.

In the Kingdom of God, you have all the grace you need to live in victory. To do so, your strongholds need to be demolished. We are bound by areas of our past, dragged with us into our new life.

Paul said that we are to "work out our salvation with fear and trembling" (Philippians 2:12). When he wrote those words, he was not referring to that moment when you prayed to receive Christ into your life. Instead, he was talking about the day-to-day salvation from conditions within us that cause us to feel defeated. When we give all we know about ourselves to our risen Lord, He works in new and powerful ways in our lives.

Now that you have established a "Listening Room" in your life, you are in a position to go to work on deliverance from the strongholds in your life. God will work in new and powerful ways in you. As a result, you will become a "young man" in the Kingdom. On page 16, you discovered that this description is given to those who have *already* "overcome the evil one." Thus, it is important that this *Arrival Kit* guides you to that victory. You are best prepared to fight the battles *without* after you have won the battles with strongholds *within* your life.

For that reason, we are going to go through the "file drawers" of your past, exposing areas that may be strongholds hindering Christ's healing. All the areas of past pain and sin are important to examine. To bring release from strongholds, we need to deal with the *root causes* of problems (sins, hurts, and curses) that are in your life today.

Consider the illustration on page 75. It demonstrates the *roots* of our lifestyles as unbelievers. That which has been experienced in the past causes the present to be distorted. We are the sum total of all our yesterdays, and carry the scars and memories with us like suitcases full of garbage.

Week 1, Ephesians 2:19 NIV
Consequently, you are no longer foreigners and aliens, but fellow citizens with God's people and members of God's household.

Week 1, 1 John 2:13 NIV
I write to you, fathers, because you have known him who is from the beginning. I write to you, young men, because you have overcome the evil one. I write to you, dear children, because you have known the Father.

Week 2, Romans 8:38-39 NIV
For I am convinced that neither death nor life, neither angels nor demons, neither the present nor the future, nor any powers, neither height nor depth, nor anything else in all creation, will be able to separate us from the love of God that is in Christ Jesus our Lord.

Week 2, Luke 17:20-21 NIV
Jesus replied, "The kingdom of God does not come visibly, nor will people say, 'Here it is,' or 'There it is,' because the kingdom of God is within you."

Week 3, Galatians 3:26-28 NIV
You are all sons of God through faith in Christ Jesus, for all of you who were baptized into Christ have clothed yourselves with Christ. There is neither Jew nor Greek, slave nor free, male nor female, for you are all one in Christ Jesus.

Week 3, Philippians 3:20-21 NIV
But our citizenship is in heaven. And we eagerly await a Savior from there, the Lord Jesus Christ, who, by the power that enables him to bring everything under his control, will transform our lowly bodies so that they will be like his glorious body.

Week 4, 1 John 4:13, 17 NIV
We know that we live in him and he in us, because he has given us of his Spirit. Love is made complete among us so that we will have confidence on the day of judgment, because in this world we are like him.

Week 4, Ephesians 2:21-22 NIV
In him the whole building is joined together and rises to become a holy temple in the Lord. And in him you too are being built together to become a dwelling in which God lives by his Spirit.

Week 5, Galatians 5:16-17 NIV
So I say, live by the Spirit, and you will not gratify the desires of the sinful nature. For the sinful nature desires what is contrary to the Spirit, and the Spirit what is contrary to the sinful nature. They are in conflict with each other, so that you do not do what you want.

Week 5, Galatians 5:22-23 NIV
But the fruit of the Spirit is love, joy, peace, patience, kindness, goodness, faithfulness, gentleness and self-control. Against such things there is no law.

Week 6, Galatians 2:20 NIV
I have been crucified with Christ and I no longer live, but Christ lives in me. The life I live in the body, I live by faith in the Son of God, who loved me and gave himself for me.

Week 6, 1 Thessalonians 5:23 NIV
May God himself, the God of peace, sanctify you through and through. May your whole spirit, soul and body be kept blameless at the coming of our Lord Jesus Christ.

Week 1
Ephesians 2:19 NIV

Week 1
1 John 2:13 NIV

Week 2
Romans 8:38-39 NIV

Week 2
Luke 17:20-21 NIV

Week 3
Galatians 3:26-28 NIV

Week 3
Philippians 3:20-21 NIV

Week 4
1 John 4:13, 17 NIV

Week 4
Ephesians 2:21-22 NIV

Week 5
Galatians 5:16-17 NIV

Week 5
Galatians 5:22-23 NIV

Week 6
Galatians 2:20 NIV

Week 6
1 Thessalonians 5:23 NIV

Week 7, 1 Corinthians 10:13 NIV
No temptation has seized you except what is common to man. And God is faithful; he will not let you be tempted beyond what you can bear. But when you are tempted, he will also provide a way out so that you can stand up under it.

Week 7, Luke 6:38 NIV
Give, and it will be given to you. A good measure, pressed down, shaken together and running over, will be poured into your lap. For with the measure you use, it will be measured to you.

Week 8, Romans 14:7-8 NIV
For none of us lives to himself alone and none of us dies to himself alone. If we live, we live to the Lord; and if we die, we die to the Lord. So, whether we live or die, we belong to the Lord.

Week 8, 1 Corinthians 9:22-23 NIV
To the weak I became weak, to win the weak. I have become all things to all men so that by all possible means I might save some. I do all this for the sake of the gospel, that I may share in its blessings.

Week 9, 2 Peter 3:9 NIV
The Lord is not slow in keeping his promise, as some understand slowness. He is patient with you, not wanting anyone to perish, but everyone to come to repentance.

Week 9, Ezekiel 18:23 NIV
Do I take any pleasure in the death of the wicked? declares the Sovereign Lord. Rather, am I not pleased when they turn from their ways and live?

Week 10, Ephesians 6:12 NIV
For our struggle is not against flesh and blood, but against the rulers, against the authorities, against the powers of this dark world and against the spiritual forces of evil in the heavenly realms.

Week 10, Ephesians 6:17-18 NIV
Take the helmet of salvation and the sword of the Spirit, which is the word of God. And pray in the Spirit on all occasions with all kinds of prayers and requests. With this in mind, be alert and always keep on praying for all the saints.

Week 11, 2 Timothy 2:11-13 NIV
Here is a trustworthy saying: If we died with him, we will also live with him; if we endure, we will also reign with him. If we disown him, he will also disown us; if we are faithless, he will remain faithful, for he cannot disown himself.

Week 11, 2 Timothy 2:15 NIV
Do your best to present yourself to God as one approved, a workman who does not need to be ashamed and who correctly handles the word of truth.

Week 7
1 Corinthians 10:13 NIV

Week 7
Luke 6:38 NIV

Week 8
Romans 14:7-8 NIV

Week 8
1 Corinthians 9:22-23 NIV

Week 9
2 Peter 3:9 NIV

Week 9
Ezekiel 18:23 NIV

Week 10
Ephesians 6:12 NIV

Week 10
Ephesians 6:17-18 NIV

Week 11
2 Timothy 2:11-13 NIV

Week 11
2 Timothy 2:15 NIV

In Ephesians 4:22, what are we to "put off?"

Our O_____ S_____, which is being

C_____ by its D_____ desires.

Paul frequently refers to our "old self." We are not released from its *presence* until we enter eternity, but we can be set free from its stranglehold on us. As we deal with strongholds, we are set free from old bondages.

There are three levels where the blood of Jesus Christ cleanses us. On the *first level*, we receive forgiveness from God in heaven (1 John 1:9). Even though we are forgiven, we may not "feel" forgiven. On the *second level*, we have a clear conscience (Acts 24:16, 1 Corinthians 4:4). It is on the *third level* that we experience cleansing and healing of the wounds *left by the effects of sin.*

Reflect on the questions below. <u>Underline</u> those that may be considered "strongholds" in your own life:

- **Do you have difficulty giving or receiving love?**
- **Do you come from a proud family? Are you proud?**
- **Are you rebellious or angry? Stubborn?**
- **Do you have unforgiveness, resentment, bitterness or hatred toward a person? Who is that person?**
- **Are you anxious or depressed?**
- **Have you ever contemplated or attempted suicide?**
- **What fears or phobias do you have?**
- **Have you visited temples? Been into witchcraft?**
- **Have you carried charms? Do you have idols?**
- **Has heavy metal or punk rock "turned you on"?**
- **Do you fantasize and lust? Masturbate?**
- **Have you been sexually molested? At what age?**
- **Do you suffer from chronic sicknesses?**
- **Do you have times of heavy doubts about the existence of God, or your own salvation?**

As you close, select 1 Corinthians 10:13 from your memory verses and begin to memorize it. *You always need it in your mind!*

Week 7, Day 2
This Unit: Personal, Please
This Week: Dealing with Strongholds
Today: "Soul ties"

Read Genesis 2:24; Matthew 19:5; 1 Corinthians 6:15-17

The term "soul tie" refers to an unhealthy uniting that takes place between two persons. It is more than "memories" or "emotions" related to another person. It is entering into a spiritual union. Soul ties can be caused by emotional or physical involvement, including sexual activity. They can be an unnatural tie to parents, friends, brothers, or sisters. You may not remember some soul ties, but they are still strongholds. Satan can work in the life through soul ties.

In Genesis 2:24 and Matthew 19:5, what soul tie is to be broken when we are married?

☐   **Submission of a person to his or her father and mother.**

☐   **Parents are not to manipulate or dominate their married children.**

☐   **Both of the above are correct.**

SOUL TIES ARE MADE IN ONE OF TWO WAYS

1. *A devotion to another person which replaces your worship and dependence on God alone.* This can develop between you and any other significant persons in your life — such as a counselor, a spouse, a boyfriend or girlfriend, or a son or daughter.

   Abraham had a soul tie to Isaac. God had to deal with it by telling him to put his son to death. In obedience, he prepared to do so. Once the soul tie had been broken by his actions, God stopped the sacrificial act. It was no longer necessary to go through with it because Abraham had restored the Lord to His rightful place on the throne of his heart.

2. *Allowing a closeness or intimacy with another person that belongs to your spouse alone.* If you are not married, this refers to physical actions belonging to the covenant relationship of marriage. If you are married, it is referring to emotions and physical actions, including sensual kissing, reserved only for your spouse. Fantasies about another person, even if there is no contact, can be a soul tie. *(If you are trapped in such a relationship, seek help from someone you can trust with your problem!)*

In 1 Corinthians 6:15-17, is intercourse with a prostitute a soul tie that continues after the activity is over, even perhaps forgotten?

☐   **Yes**   ☐   **No**   ☐   **Unsure**

TWO THINGS HAPPEN IN A SOUL TIE

1. *Sin is committed.* An individual experiences guilty feelings and true guilt before God. This establishes a stronghold for Satan to plague us.
2. *Spiritual bonding takes place.* We are spiritually tied to everyone with whom we have established a soul tie. Adultery, for example, creates a stronghold bringing inner confusion, making it hard to bond with your spouse. We are still connected to the other person. This has a potent effect on us. David's sin with Bathsheba brought him endless anguish.

Sometimes the soul tie may be to a person loved long ago who is still recalled in fantasies. If any relationship becomes more important than having a single-minded heart before the Lord, *it's a stronghold. You will face constant defeat!*

HOW DO WE BREAK SOUL TIES?

They must be dealt with as sin (1 John 1:9). Deal with each one separately. This includes *confession*: naming the sin specifically, renouncing not only the sin but also all the pleasure gained from it. It is important for you to share your confession with another person (1 Thessalonians 5:11).

Then, there is *cleansing*: bring the sin under the blood of Jesus, receive forgiveness, and stay in the "Listening Room" until your spirit knows God has cleansed you.

Finally, there is *contemplation*. What motivated that soul tie to be established? Was it loneliness? Curiosity about sex? Anger, and a determination to hurt someone else? Once you have discerned what triggered you to act in that way, a liberation from the stronghold will take place, and Satan will not have entry to entice you again.

Meditate on Colossians 1:13-14: *"For he has rescued us from the dominion of darkness and brought us into the kingdom of the Son he loves, in whom we have redemption, the forgiveness of sins."*

It may help you to see in your imagination the connection between yourself and the person with whom the soul tie has been made. Then, using the powerful name of Jesus, declare He has broken the tie. Place your hand on your heart and verbally *give back* every part of the person with whom the soul tie has been made. Finally, *take back* every part of your own life from the person involved.

Pray: "I am free. I am forgiven. I am cleansed from (name of person) forever through Christ Jesus!"

WHEN YOU CAN'T DO IT BY YOURSELF . . .

Many times, those who seek to deal with soul ties need the ministry of a Spirit-filled believer who is sensitive to others and discerning through prayer. If you face a soul tie that has such a stronghold on you that you cannot break it alone, by all means seek out a spiritual companion for your journey. It may be your mentor, your cell leader, or a person on the pastoral team whom you trust.

God provides people who are "called alongside to help" us in our Kingdom journey. Don't be afraid to share with a suitable person: *"But encourage one another daily, as long as it is called Today, so that none of you may be hardened by sin's deceitfulness"* (Hebrews 3:13).

(This week's materials is adapted from unpublished work by John Deel Griffin, Titusville, FL, USA)

Week 7, Day 3
This Unit: Personal, Please
This Week: Dealing with Strongholds
Today: Dealing with Idolatry

Read Exodus 20:3-5; 1 John 5:21; Galatians 5:19-21

Too often we gloss over the First Commandment, considering it to be the easiest of the ten to keep. That's not true! God said plainly, *"You shall have no other gods before me. You shall not make for yourself an idol in the form of anything in heaven above or on the earth beneath or in the waters below. You shall not bow down to them or worship them; for I, the Lord your God, am a jealous God, punishing the children for the sin of the fathers to the third and fourth generation of those who hate me, . . ."*

In Singapore, idol worshippers comprise a large segment of the Chinese population. Many homes have a "god shelf" with images of Buddha, Quan Yin, Hanemun, etc. Tourists sometime foolishly purchase these items as souvenirs and take them home.

Why does God detest idols so much, bringing punishment on the children for the sin of their fathers who worship them? The answer is found in Romans 1. Paul explains that God has revealed His power and majesty to all men through His creation. However, men said to themselves, "If I accept the truth of God's existence, the logical thing will be to bow down and worship Him. Then I must surrender my life to His authority. *I will not do it!"* The fierce determination of humanity to remain in a lawless condition is their motivation for making idols. Knowing they are superior to the gods they manufacture, people can manipulate them, flattering them to do what they think will bring them "good luck," making their wishes come true.

They *"exchanged the glory of the immortal God for images made to look like mortal man and birds and animals and reptiles" (Romans 1:23)*. Every idol is a bold statement made by the owners that the authority of God has been flatly rejected. This act will not go unpunished! It breaks the First Commandment.

Many times a Chinese person has said to me, "I cannot become a Christian for fear of offending my parents. They worship idols." Each time I hear this, I remember that the curse of idols goes down to the *"third and fourth generation,"* damning scores of people to an eternal hell because they have been raised in an idol-worshipping home which presses them to follow family traditions!

I have attended several idol-smashing and god-shelf burning ceremonies. Those who worship idols also collect charms, which are forgotten about, in dresser drawers. Permission is given to the members of the cell group to "cleanse the house" of all these things. They are found and destroyed, with praises sung to God.

WHEREVER THERE IS AN IDOL, THERE IS A STRONGHOLD

When a family purchases an idol, they take it to a temple to be infused with the presence of a spirit. Thus, families eat and sleep in the presence of demons. Their power darkens minds, brings fear and superstition, and imprisons those in the family. A true member of the Kingdom of God will not allow idols on his property, regardless of the uproar it may cause among the relatives. The entire Old Testament is filled with God's anger toward those who go *"embracing other gods."* He sees a Christian who allows idols as committing spiritual adultery!

One of the most dangerous things about idols is their power to deceive. Satan is anxious to blind eyes and deafen ears. The deception of those who live with idols is that *they never realize how evil their idols are in God's sight!* If they realized the wrath of God toward these demon-infested objects, they would recoil from them as though they were being attacked by a snake.

ALL IDOLS ARE NOT OBVIOUS

Among Webster's definitions for "idol" is this one: *"the object of excessive attachment, admiration, or infatuation."* Thus, idolatry is the most common sin among those who live in the western world as well as in the oriental world.

Satan is not only a liar and a deceiver — He's also *smart!* For those who are "sophisticated," he provides a different set of idols. They are *"objects of excessive attachment."* For one person, the idol may be a fine automobile. For another, it may be a house. Idols may be travel, a sport (either practiced or observed), an ambition, a hobby, an art. *Always* these idols are considered not only to be *safe*, but to also bring *comfort* to the worshipper. For others, Satan offers drugs, alcohol, gambling, or promiscuity.

LET'S FACE THE ISSUE SQUARELY . . .

If you have glossed over a stronghold of idolatry that is in your life, this is the time to deal with it! *God can set you free.* His power is available to you. The first step is to go to the "Listening Room" and talk to the Master. Ask Him to release you from any deception that has blinded you from seeing your idols as evil. Be honest with yourself. *Are you in the bondage to an excessive attachment?*

In 1 Samuel 15, God spoke through Samuel the prophet. God promised to bless Israel as they went into battle against their enemy, the Amalekites. God ordered the Israelites to destroy every person and object in the Amalekite tribe. *(God knew allowing the "bad" to mingle with the "good" would ultimately lead to the corruption of everyone!)* Instead of obeying God, King Saul preserved treasures and spared the life of evil King Agag. Samuel was so furious! Because of his disobedience, Saul lost his throne. Agag was put to death. There could be no compromise.

If you have an idol in your heart or your life, be aware that you have a stronghold for Satan to enter and leave you as he desires. You will never know victory in your life, and the peace of God will always elude you. *Utterly destroy your false object of worship!*

Some years ago, our family went to Vietnam as missionaries. An old veteran from Asia told us, "As you go, hold your possessions in your *hand*, not in your *heart*." We were only there for a few weeks before Saigon was overrun. Many missionaries left without any of their possessions. We often recalled the advice we received. I would like to give some to you: *Destroy your idols. Hold what is in your heart in your hand instead. Do not compromise by allowing idols to control you.*

🖋 **It's time to go to the "Listening Room." What idols might you be worshipping instead of God?**

Week 7, Day 4
This Unit: Personal, Please
This Week: Dealing with Strongholds
Today: Treasures on Earth

Read Luke 16:19-31; Matthew 6:19-23

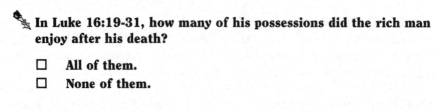 **In Luke 16:19-31, how many of his possessions did the rich man enjoy after his death?**

☐   **All of them.**
☐   **None of them.**

One day I was walking through the oldest section of Singapore, seeking to learn more about the culture. I saw a shop house where men were making items out of bamboo sticks and paper. A replica of a half-size Mercedes Benz caught my eyes, complete with paper seats and a steering wheel. There was a brightly painted castle, five feet tall, with furniture included. There was also a paper maché doll, nearly life-size, of an extremely curvaceous blonde woman dressed in a voluptuous manner.

Someone told me that these toy-like objects were for the use of a poor taxi driver who had just died. As his body was to be cremated, these paper figures would all be burned nearby for his use in the "afterlife." He had been watching rich men all his life, and he was determined to enjoy some of their pleasures, even if it had to happen in his non-existent "world of ghosts."

A major world religion describes heaven as a place of endless fulfillment of lusts, where unbridled sensualism takes place forever. In the future Kingdom of God, such is not the case.

In Matthew 6:19-23, Jesus spoke of *"treasures on earth"* and *"treasures in heaven."* Exactly what are the "treasures in heaven"? What are these future "kingdom treasures" we should value? If we know the answer to that question, *we will live this life in a special way.* Jesus said, *"For where your treasure is, there your heart will be also."*

The treasures on earth are easy to list. They all revolve around the one word: *"Treasure."* What do you treasure the most? People treasure different things. The list of what is treasured is endless, but *what* we treasure is not as important as the heart attitudes that give something high priority.

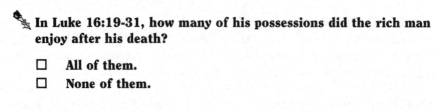 **What or who do you treasure most right now? Let's review the list we considered earlier (page 33), which appears on page 81. Imagine you have just died. You have just entered your "afterlife" in the kingdom of God. Without turning back to see what you wrote earlier, prioritize the list again, with "1" being the highest, "18" being the lowest. Take your time. Think carefully about what you would treasure when life as you now live it is finished.**

Your heart follows your treasures. Avoid placing your affections and loyalties on personal possessions. In Mark 10:21, we are told that Jesus looked at the rich young ruler *"and loved him"* as He said, *"One thing you lack. Go, sell everything you have and give to the poor, and you will have treasure in heaven. Then come, follow me."*

Let the words *"and loved him"* sink deep into your spirit! Jesus knew how badly this young man was swindling himself by treasuring earthly wealth. He knew he had to sell un-necessary or distracting possessions and give the money to the poor or to the Lord's work before his life could be enriched.

In the original Greek, the word for "money" in Matthew 6:24 is "mammon." Jesus says love for money is the worship of a demonic spirit. Money must be used wisely, for it can blind us to reality and destroy our true devotion to God.

As you consider the issue of treasure, I want to give you a principle that Ruth and I have sought to live by for over 41 years. We lovingly share it for your use:

MY VALUE SYSTEM, PART 2

I HAVE JUST DIED. THIS IS WHAT I NOW VALUE:

PRIORITY   VALUE

_____ Being prosperous, wealthy

_____ Doing exciting things

_____ Accomplishing something big

_____ Living without conflict

_____ Feeling equal with others

_____ Making my family secure

_____ Free to make my own choices

_____ Being happy, contented

_____ Avoiding inner conflicts

_____ Having close friends

_____ Being safe from crime

_____ Enjoying life (travel, movies, etc.)

_____ Doing the will of God

_____ Having self-respect, self-esteem

_____ Being recognized and admired

_____ Closeness, intimacy with others

_____ Making good decisions

_____ Desire for power

It is the task of a servant to obey his Master.

It is the obligation of the Master to provide for that servant.

Therefore, the servant need never be afraid!

Week 7, Day 5
This Unit: Personal, Please
This Week: Dealing with Strongholds
Today: "Just Do It!"

Read 2 Corinthians 6:1-2; Philippians 1:6, 2:12-13

In 2 Corinthians 6:1, to whom was Paul writing?

☐   **Fellow Christians**

☐   **Those who had not yet become Christians**

In 2 Corinthians 6:2, is the "day of salvation" speaking of the initial salvation we receive at the time we ask Christ to enter our lives?

☐   **Yes**

☐   **No**

☐   **Unsure**

If you had difficulty knowing how to answer that last question, always remember these important verses found in Philippians 1:6 and 2:12-13: *"being confident of this, that he who began a good work in you will carry it on to completion until the day of Christ Jesus . . . . Therefore, my dear friends, as you have always obeyed — not only in my presence, but now much more in my absence — continue to work out your salvation with fear and trembling, for it is God who works in you to will and to act according to his good purpose."*

YOUR SALVATION IS IN THREE STAGES
1. At the cross, you were set free from the penalty of sin.
2. Day by day, you are being set free from the power of sin.
3. In the future, you will be set free from the presence of sin.

Thus, the passages you are meditating upon today are written to you for *today*, encouraging you to be released from the power of sin. For you, "now is the day of salvation!"

Remember that the word "sin" refers to the proud 'I' that desires to reign over your life, and not just the "sins," or actions, which are caused by that proud 'I'. If you enthrone Jesus Christ in your life and present to Him the strongholds you have admitted exist in your values, your habits, and your lifestyle, you will be set free from them by His power.

Even more significant, each victory you experience within *your own life* will make it possible for you to begin to engage in the spiritual warfare going on in *the world around you*! You see, we are not to be so egocentric that we continually think only of ourselves and our own needs. We are to be healed persons who can bring the power of our Lord to revive others!

I have fought a battle with my weight all my life. (If you have a similar problem, you have my sympathy!) Finally, my doctor told me I had developed a form of diabetes that afflicts older people. She said, "You have a choice. You can either let your diabetes destroy you, or you can exercise an hour a day and change your diet." I had to face reality. I had ignored exercise for years; now it was time to face the consequences. I joined an exercise club, and as I began my first miserable hour of walking around the track as hard as I could push myself, a frail, little lass of 24 or so passed me like I was a stationary object. How humiliating! Worst of all, when she finally got six or eight feet ahead of me, I saw the words printed in bright red on the back of her T-shirt. They said, *"JUST DO IT!"*

I said, "Lord, you have spoken in the past through thunder and lightning and a still, small voice. This is the first time I have heard your message on the back of a T-shirt!"

It's time for you to retire to the "Listening Room." Perhaps for several days you have been arguing with yourself about some of the strongholds the Spirit has brought to your attention. You have said, "I can't find deliverance from these areas. I have tried before, and I hate feeling defeated when I fail."

Now, who do you think planted those thoughts in your mind? Did they come from the Holy Spirit? Of course not! Are you learning to recognize not only the voice of God, but also the whispers of Satan? Can you identify the sources of your thoughts?

Listen! Do you hear the Spirit of God? Is He saying, "Your past problems in gaining victory have come through your trying to do what only I can do. Quit trying! Present your life to Me as a living sacrifice. I have all power in heaven and earth, and deliverance is yours when I am in control.

"For it is God who works in you to will and to act according to His good purpose."

Week 8, Day 1
This Unit: Personal, Please
This Week: Dealing with Attitudes
Today: Happiness Is a Choice!

Read Matthew 5:3-12

> **How would you define "happiness?" (Tick the boxes that fit your personal definition:)**
>
> ☐   Being content with my circumstances
> ☐   Living in a beautiful house
> ☐   Being with someone I love or admire
> ☐   Pleasurable meals with good friends
> ☐   Not being under pressure
> ☐   Taking a long rest by the seaside
> ☐   Feeling pleased with my accomplishments
> ☐   Other: (specify)_____

Have you ever had a waiter place gourmet food on your table and say, *"Enjoy!"*? How did you react to that single word? Did it make you feel a bit uneasy, knowing that a single meal could not bring you much long-term pleasure? *Was the waiter's comment based on a premise that happiness could be found on a plate?*

The late Redd Harper used to tell about walking down an Oklahoma road and meeting a man with a sour look on his face. Redd asked, "What's the matter with you?" The man said, "Ain't you seen the papers? Those foreigners are gonna come over here with an atom bomb and blow us all to hell!" Redd laughed and said, "Speak for yourself! If they drop a bomb on me, it'll blow me *all the way to heaven!*"

In the kingdoms of this world, we are carefully brainwashed to believe that happiness is found in our *surroundings*. In the Kingdom of God, happiness is found instead in a *relationship*.

Matthew 5:3-12 gives us the secret of happiness. Let's think about this:

The poor in spirit are happy because they have relinquished their need to impress others. They know their significance does not come from what they accomplish but from the fact that they are children of God!

Those who mourn does not refer to those who have lost a loved one, but rather to those who are truly sorry for past sins and have given themselves completely to their Lord.

The meek are not those who are weaklings; rather, they are like lambs, having no defense. They totally rely upon their Shepherd for protection.

Those who hunger and thirst for righteousness are happy because they have discovered an important principle: Jesus alone is righteous, and He dwells inside all believers. Jesus is their righteousness. They don't have to try to keep a set of rules in order for God to love them; they simply enjoy their fellowship with the indwelling Christ.

Those who are merciful are happy because they have discovered how much joy there is in being compassionate and sympathetic to others.

Those who are pure in heart are happy because they don't carry around a lot of guilt from impure thoughts and deeds.

Those who make peace are happy because they bring the Prince of Peace to those who are miserable.

Those who are persecuted, insulted, and falsely accused are happy because each event assures them that unbelievers identify them as true followers of Christ.

When we live in the Kingdom of God, our circumstances no longer control our happiness. Instead, our life in Christ brings us the "peace that passes understanding."

🌹 **Happiness is a choice. How do you see the glass in this illustration?**

☐   **It is half full.**

☐   **It is half empty.**

🌹 **Do you think those who see it as half empty rather than half full have a problem with being happy? Why, or why not?**

Some people are never happy. Others are *occasionally* happy. Still others seem to have a constant joy in their countenance, that radiates to all they meet.

🌹 **Which description best fits you?**

☐   **People seldom see me smile. I probably am not thought of as a happy person.**

☐   **People usually see me smiling and happy.**

☐   **People don't know what to expect. I have mood swings. I don't always know myself how I am going to react.**

🌹 **How do you desire to be seen by others?**

☐   **As a joyful, happy person.**

☐   **As a serious, unhappy person.**

☐   **As a moody person.**

If you are not sure of the way others view you (happy or unhappy), why not discuss the matter in your cell group, or with your mentor? There is no reason to live with a spirit of fear, of dread, or of worry. One of your rights as a citizen of the Kingdom of God is to overcome the attacks of Satan which make you unhappy. Remember — at the root of every attitude there is a *spiritual condition*. Our lives are always linked to the presence of the indwelling Christ. He has come to bring us *His joy, His peace, His happiness*. Spend a moment in the "Listening Room" as you meditate on today's Scripture. *Listen for His word to you.*

Week 8, Day 2
This Unit: Personal, Please
This Week: Dealing with Attitudes
Today: What About Sexual Impurity?

Read Matthew 5:27-30; 1 Corinthians 6:9-10; John 8:12

✎ **According to Matthew 5:27-30, is secret lust less serious than actually having intercourse with someone?**

☐ **Adultery is more serious.**

☐ **Secret lust is more serious.**

☐ **The two actions are equally serious.**

☐ **It's impossible not to lust!**

Do you know the difference between *adultery* and *fornication*? *Adultery* is sexual intercourse between a married person and someone who is not his or her spouse. *Fornication* is sex between two unmarried people.

1 Corinthians 6:9,10 contain harsh words! What did Paul mean when he wrote that adulterers and fornicators will not *"inherit the kingdom of God"*? The word *"inherit"* means "to have a share in" the reign of God. To put it another way, the person who has an improper relationship with another person will suffer a terrible loss!

God has no part in lust, fornication, or adultery. In His sight, a look or a touch of lust cannot happen when He is reigning over us. When we permit such actions, we are not living in His Kingdom. We are on our own!

Through the years, my heart has been broken by the discovery of immoral conduct among Christians. Yet, who among us has not been tantalized by thoughts or situations leading to sexual impurity?

I have been told, "It is not possible for a human being to live without lust. It is a natural part of the emotional life, and to suppress it will make a person neurotic." If that is true, then Jesus was wrong to teach us the truths in these verses.

Years ago, I took a group of students from a seminary on an around-the-world summer "classroom." These were all fine men, most of whom were married, and who were all headed for the mission field. At the end of five weeks, we had a farewell gathering. I asked, "What has been the greatest spiritual battle you have faced during our time together?" Most shared the same thing: "I have fought lust the entire time."

Is the temptation to be sexually impure a typical problem in the Kingdom of God? Yes. But the words of Jesus and Paul are very clear. Those who lust or commit sexual acts *have no share in His reign*.

Every time those men travelled around Asia, they saw girls and women dressed in a way that exposed their bodies and shape for all to see. To make things even worse, in an unfamiliar culture, *people* become *objects*. Thus, these fine Christian men were in a battle. Would they view these women as *objects* or *persons*? Lust is always based on this issue. So is adultery and fornication. Those who have sex born out of objectification are simply using the other person for self-satisfaction, without concern for that person's true self.

There is absolutely no place in the Kingdom of God for people who use and abuse others, making them objects to be enjoyed! When a woman gets on a bus dressed in a way to expose her body for all to see, *what does Jesus see?*

A man who sees through the eyes of his Lord will pray: "Lord, that lady is your child. You died for her! You meant for her to be loved and respected as a *person, not an object*. You intended for her to know true affection from a man who would cherish her and represent You as her husband. Father, I may never know her name, but I ask you to give her a strong desire for You."

Jesus has said, "If your eye can't see the real person, *pluck out that eye!*" In other words, replace your eyes with *His* eyes. When He met a woman who had been through five marriages and now lived with a man who was not her husband, He showed us how He treated those who could easily be used for personal satisfaction (see John 4:7-26). He lives in us — and when He is in charge of what we see and how we touch, the Kingdom of God is present.

**It's time to enter the "Listening Room." As you do so,
memorize or review 1 Corinthians 10:13.**

Week 8, Day 3
This Unit: Personal, Please
This Week: Dealing with Attitudes
Today: Your Weaker Brother

Read Romans 14:1-15

🖋 **Situation: You are attending a cell group that includes a new believer who has smoked for years. You feel strongly that our bodies are the temples of the Holy Spirit, and this habit should not be tolerated. In a cell group discussion about it, this person said, "I don't see anything wrong with smoking. It's a personal matter." Which of the following actions would you probably take?**

☐ Give the person a carton of cigarettes for a birthday present.

☐ Treat the matter as none of your business.

☐ Insist the person stop smoking, or not return to the cell group.

☐ Pray much about the matter, and say nothing.

☐ Offer to mentor the person and meet weekly to review *The Arrival Kit*.

One of the curses of religion is a legalistic list of "do's" and "don'ts." In this passage, Paul tells us that we are all going to stand before the Lord and be judged, but we have no right to judge one another.

In the Kingdom of God, there are some things that are *always wrong*. This includes fornication and adultery. There are other things that are *always right*. This includes spending time in the "Listening Room" and caring for hurting people. There are also areas relating to *doubtful things*, which are not expressly endorsed or forbidden in Scripture. How are we to act towards one another?

TWO PRINCIPLES ARE PROVIDED

The first principle is *my liberty to live as pleases the Lord* (Romans 14:6). I am a child *(PAIS)* of the King. I am not under bondage to my fellow Christian. I am free to wear my hair long or short, to observe certain holidays or to ignore them. In Romans 14:12, I know that one day I will face the Lord and account for my lifestyle. If I abuse His blessings on my life by living lavishly, for example, I will have to answer to Him. No one has a right to control my decisions about *doubtful things*.

The second principle is *my need to walk in love toward my fellow Christian* (Romans 14:15). If I demand my freedom to live in a certain way, I no longer walk in love. Therefore, there are some situations in which I must give up my *freedom* as an act of love for my brother or sister in Christ.

Years ago, I pastored a church in Pensacola, Florida. I would often take the young people to the beach for a barbeque. We would meet at the church and drive several cars to our favorite swimming area. After doing so on a Saturday, I preached on Sunday morning. When the service was over, I went to the door to shake hands with the people who were leaving.

One of my favorite "grannies" was Mama Mayo, who was in her 80s. On that particular Sunday, she refused to greet me or shake my hand. Alarmed, I followed her to the street and asked, "Mama Mayo, what's wrong?" Tears welled out from her eyes as she said, "I can never listen to you preach again. I never thought I would see my pastor wearing short pants in public!"

Only then did I recall wearing beach shorts as we packed the food into my car in front of the church auditorium. Without realizing it, I had offended my aged friend. "Mama," I said sadly, "I ask your forgiveness. I did not realize that would offend you. I promise you that never again will you see me wearing short pants!"

From that time forward in Pensacola, the only time I wore shorts was when I was actually at the seashore. Mama Mayo meant far more to me than my conscience-free right to dress casually. There came a day when the Mayo family flew me back to preach the funeral service for that dear saint. As I stood by her casket, I was so glad I had limited my freedom by *agape* love.

Belonging to a cell group will cause you to rub against other Christians who may not see eye-to-eye with you about doubtful things. Consider them to be "heavenly sandpaper" to cause you to see the difference between doing as you please and doing what pleases others — and your Lord!

It's "Listening Room" time! Use the checklist in the next column to guide your sharing and your hearing from your Lord.

FOR SELF-EXAMINATION

- Does what I eat cause another person to stumble?
- Does what I drink cause another person to stumble?
- Do I have habits that seem proper to me, yet grieve others who watch me?
- Am I presently the victim of another person or group who demands a certain conduct, and who is robbing me of my liberty in Christ?
- Am I sensitive to others, and how my life is impacting them?
- Jesus said, "But if anyone causes one of these little ones who believe in me to sin, it would be better for him to have a large millstone hung around his neck and to be drowned in the depths of the sea" (Matthew 18:6). Am I sensitive to the needs of the spiritual "children" in my cell group? Does my use of personal freedom in Christ offend or cause them to stumble?

PRAYER:

"Lord Jesus, make me sensitive to others. Let my life be a blessing in all that I do or say. Let my spirit know how You want to love through me, and give me more and more of Your love for others. I choose Your will in place of my own will in every circumstance of my life. Amen."

Week 8, Day 4
This Unit: Personal, Please
This Week: Dealing with Attitudes
Today: Your "Pecking Order"

Read 1 Corinthians 9:19-23; Galatians 3:28; James 2:1-10

The term "pecking order" comes from watching chickens eat food. They establish among themselves a "head rooster" who eats first. There is a special "order" for the rest to "peck" at the edibles.

In the kingdoms of this world, humans also establish a "pecking order." Frequently, light-skinned people look down on dark-skinned people. A Korean friend of mine had a terrible time trying to rent a place to live in Tokyo. In the Japanese mind, Koreans are "beneath them." In many languages of the world, there are actually *three different vocabularies* to be learned: one to address your superiors, another to address your equals, and another to address your inferiors.

On a visit to Korea, I had calling cards with the title of "Executive Secretary" of our ministry. In America, that is a worthy title — but Korean pastors were very confused by it. They could not decide whether I was above them or below them!

It's an ugly thing to hear someone comment, *"But would you want your daughter to marry a _____?"* Satan delights in divisions among us, and all his kingdoms have established very special "pecking orders." We are all the victims!

REVIEWING YOUR RESPONSIBILITY

Do you remember our discussion of human categories based on the report of a famous Polish sociologist? She divided people into three groups:

1. The "People" People — These are persons we consider to be "on our level" or above us. We feel comfortable being with them and are willing to confide in them. They are socially, intellectually, and economically in our category. We enjoy being with them. We often make special places for those who are richer than we are, hoping they will part with some of their wealth and make us richer than we are *(see James 2:1-10)*.

2. The "Machine" People — These are people we do not wish to associate with on a social or personal basis, but we need their services. They include the woman at the bank who cashes our checks and the man who repairs our car. Being polite to them, even asking them about their families, is considered a way to "oil them up" and make them work harder for us. However, we do not really care about them. If they ever asked for a loan or a favor, we would find many excuses to eliminate them from our list of "machines" who perform tasks for us.

3. The "Landscape" People — These are the people who do not fit the first two classes. We do not have any interest in them and would consider it a bother to invest time or concern on them. They are simply part of the "landscape" as we pass by them on the street or share an elevator ride with them. They are worthless to us.

Go in-depth with the Bible verses for today. Follow the directions below.

Read 1 Corinthians 9:19-23 and then answer this question:
What is the main point of this passage?

_____

Read Galatians 3:28 and then answer this question:
What does this verse say about "pecking order?"

_____

Read James 2:2-4 and then answer this question:
How are we warned against discriminating in our cell group meetings?

_____

This next activity is for your "Listening Room." Think about the people in your *oikos*. List the way you treat them: are they People, Machines, or Landscape to you? Write their names in the spaces provided. Circle "P," "M," or "L," as appropriate, for each person:

1. Those in your immediate family, including brothers and sisters:

_____ P M L _____ P M L
_____ P M L _____ P M L
_____ P M L _____ P M L

2. Those in the place where you work or study:

_____ P M L _____ P M L
_____ P M L _____ P M L
_____ P M L _____ P M L

3. Those in your cell group:

_____ P M L _____ P M L
_____ P M L _____ P M L
_____ P M L _____ P M L
_____ P M L _____ P M L
_____ P M L _____ P M L

How does the Christ in you desire for them to be treated?

Week 8, Day 5
This Unit: Personal, Please
This Week: Dealing with Attitudes
Today: Who's Hurting Whom?

Read Ephesians 4:30-32

🖋 **In what way do you think the attitudes mentioned in verse 31 grieve the Holy Spirit? Check your answer(s):**

☐   He is not a participant in such attitudes.

☐   He is not the source of such attitudes.

☐   Because he indwells us, he must bear the pain caused by such attitudes.

☐   These attitudes destroy our joy and peace.

☐   All of the above are correct.

The word for *"grieve"* used in this Scripture means *"vexed"* or *"distressed."* Can you identify with those emotions? Can you recall a moment of great grief in your own life, and how you ached within?

Has someone you dearly loved died? You recall your grief was heavy because of your strong feelings for that person, and also because you felt the pain of being separated.

The Holy Spirit within us suffers such inner pain when we choose to release these strong feelings into our spirits. Paul says, "Get rid of them! They are breaking the heart of the One Who has come to dwell within you."

SIX WRETCHED ATTITUDES

Let's examine the six attitudes in this verse:

All Bitterness — The word refers to an acid-like poison that eats away at all which surrounds it. Bitterness is the hatred that is nourished by constantly reliving past experiences when we were victimized. The question never answered by a bitter person is, *"Who is being destroyed by my hatred? Does it do any damage to the person who caused it?"* In every case, the answer will be the same. The acid is eating away at the insides of the person who is bitter, not the other party. Satan's deception blocks the bitter mind from recognizing that fact! The results of bitterness can include physical breakdowns, emotional disturbances, and twisted logic. *Worst of all, the Holy Spirit is grieved and, in effect, helpless before it!*

Rage and Anger — *Rage* describes a deep, destructive passion. *Anger* refers to a desire to destroy, to hurt. It is the next layer above *bitterness*, and causes actions designed to destroy. That which is buried deep within is coming to the surface!

Brawling and Slander — *Brawling* comes from a Greek word meaning *"screaming out with a growling voice."* It can be likened to the sound of a lion's roar as it pounces on its prey. Bitterness has erupted past desire to hurt. Now there is outward action called *"slander."* Slander refers to a deep inner resentment causing words to come forth which are intended to destroy someone. Whether the slander is based on fact or fancy is of no concern to the speaker; the intention is to cut, hurt, and destroy!

Every Form of Malice — *Malice* describes an evil intention to destroy the worth of another person. It refers to a *way of life*, a fixation on doing everything possible to ruin another person.

THIS COMBINATION OF EMOTIONS IS COMMONPLACE

In the kingdoms of this world, men enjoy observing the cycle of these attitudes so much that they read novels and watch movies built upon this theme! Evil feeds on evil, and society becomes more and more corrupted by the downward spiral.

Do you live with bitterness in your heart? I am thinking of a bitter woman who was molested as a child by her father. I am remembering a man in our cell group whose father promised him for years that he would inherit his factory and then sold it and pocketed the money. The stories of people being cheated and abused are endless. Employers fire long-term, faithful employees so they will not have to give them a pension. Everywhere we look, there are many reasons for people to feel bitter.

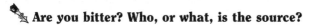 **Are you bitter? Who, or what, is the source?**

Have you come to terms with its destructive power in your life? Are you prepared for God to release you from this stronghold?

The instruction in verse 31 is very clear. Get rid of these things — *"JUST DO IT!"* It is breathtaking to realize Paul says *we must take the first step.* Passively wallowing in self-pity will not solve the problem.

The Holy Spirit is watching, grieving, and weeping as He waits for us to make a decision to put an end to these attitudes. The moment we make the decision to act decisively, He responds to our cry for help. He is then able to "come alongside to help" *(that's the literal meaning of the word "Comforter").* Once you take the first step, He is no longer alienated. You restore Him to His rightful place in your heart, and all things change.

Ask yourself: "Whom am I destroying by my attitudes?" Put yourself at the top of the list. Quit justifying yourself by saying, "I have a right to feel this way! I am not imagining all this. I bear the scars of it all!" That may be true, but *you* are the one who has refused to let the wound heal, aren't you? Who else is being destroyed? Your friends? Your family? Those you influence the most? Remember a bitter spirit spreads its acidic poison into all it touches.

In the Kingdom of God, we have two outstanding examples to remember: Jesus and Stephen. Both shared the same spirit as they were wrongly murdered: *"Father, forgive them. They don't know what they are doing!"* When you invite the Holy Spirit to "come alongside to help," you will find that Jesus responds to your hurt with His love and forgiveness.

Do you need help? Your cell group will listen.
Share with all, or with your mentor.
Now, it's "Listening Room" time . . .

Week 9, Day 1
This Unit: Facing the Powers
This Week: The Battle for Men's Souls
Today: The Heart of God

Read 2 Peter 3:9; Isaiah 30:18; Ezekiel 18:23, 33:11; Romans 2:4

Entering the Kingdom of God does not mean withdrawing from the presence of evil and unbelief. I have often smiled as I have read about the way God directed Abraham. Hebrews 11:8-10 tells us he was *looking for a city built by God* when he left his homeland to journey hundreds of miles to the west.

Finally, God said, "Abraham, you have arrived. This is where I want you to live." He took one look around him and might have replied, "*Here*, God? This isn't exactly what I expected. You know the purpose of my journey. I just want to be closer to You. I left my family and friends behind to be with You. This doesn't look like the place to do that! Lord, I've been looking around, and this place is *wicked*! There are carvings of sexual organs all over the hillsides. These Canaanites sacrifice virgins and burn babies alive to their pagan idols. I expected for you to lead me to a remote mountain retreat or perhaps to the seaside. *Do you really mean to put me here?*"

HOW ODD OF GOD!

Not at all! If Abraham had known more about God, he would have realized how logical it was for him to be put there. Ezekiel 33:11 says, *"As surely as I live, declares the Sovereign Lord, I take no pleasure in the death of the wicked, but rather that they turn from their ways and live. Turn! Turn from your evil ways!"*

Why did God send Abraham to the Canaanites? For the same reason He sent His Son to live among us. His kindness and His compassion are revealed in the Bible, to be sure. However, a *human body*, the body of Christ, brought God's Spirit into the darkest, most evil places. Salvation comes to us in the human form of Christ, Who brought the Kingdom of God to evil men.

> **In 2 Peter 3:9, what are we told about God's attitude toward unbelievers?**
>
> ☐ He is patient with their rebellious lifestyle.
> ☐ He is looking forward to destroying all who are unrepentant with a consuming fire.
> ☐ Both of the above statements are true.
> ☐ Neither of the above statements is true.

You may meet someone who believes a massive lie. He will say that the God of the Old Testament was a God of wrath, and by the beginning of the New Testament, men had decided to make Him gentler. That's nonsense! In addition to the Ezekiel passage, consider Isaiah's statement about God: *"Yet the Lord longs to be gracious to you; he rises to show you compassion. For the Lord is a God of justice. Blessed are all who wait for him!"* This powerful truth permeates the Kingdom of Heaven. In our hearts, where He dwells, we should sense *compassion* rising within us toward unbelievers. In Romans 2:4, we are told of *"the riches of His kindness, tolerance and patience."* The reason? *"God's kindness leads . . . toward repentance."*

The Arrival Kit is written to help you understand the value systems present in the Kingdom of Heaven. At the top of the priorities, the values, is the need for all men to be told that *God's kindness leads toward repentance!*

🖋 **Have you ever considered what God values the most? Rank the ten areas below in order of importance from 1 to 10:**

_____ **To see His son loved and honored.**

_____ **To establish His kingdom among us.**

_____ **To guide us by His perfect will.**

_____ **To provide for our daily needs.**

_____ **To deliver us from temptation.**

_____ **To receive our worship and praise.**

_____ **To bring justice to all men.**

_____ **To give His righteousness to us.**

_____ **To plant His spirit within us.**

_____ **To bring eternal salvation to all men through His son's death on the cross.**

As you were completing the previous exercise, did you say to yourself, "This is ridiculous! How can *anyone* rank the order of God's priorities?" While you had to do a lot of speculation, there is no question about what our Father's *number one priority is: It is to bring eternal salvation to all men through His Son's death on the cross.* Did you select that as "1"?

That truth is made clear by *all* of the books of the Bible, from Genesis to Revelation! The all-consuming passion of His heart is to bring *all men* to know His love, forgiveness, and fellowship.

🖋 **Since that is true, what does He desire for you to do while you live on this earth? (Check all answers you believe to be correct.)**

☐ **Withdraw socially from all unbelievers. Have friendships with Christians only.**

☐ **Live among those who need to be rescued from the curse of Satan's domination.**

☐ **Bring many unreached people to join us in His wonderful kingdom.**

☐ **Enjoy God to the fullest and ignore the suffering of broken lives around us.**

This day's material is created to help you face this fact: *The love of God for all men means our first priority as Christians is to point people to the Cross.* To make that our Number One value can be the greatest shakeup we will ever experience in our lifestyles. Do you agree? *It's time to visit the "Listening Room!"*

Week 9, Day 2
This Unit: Facing the Powers
This Week: The Battle for Men's Souls
Today: The Heart of Satan

Read John 8:44; 2 Corinthians 4:3-4; 1 John 5:19

When athletic teams prepare to play against one another, they watch videotapes of previous games played by their opponents. Those teams know the more they can learn about their adversaries, the stronger they will play in the competition.

We have examined the heart of God, and we know He wants *all men* to be delivered from Satan's control. As soldiers of the Cross, we should know the Devil's tactics.

One of the most powerful descriptions of Satan is found in John 8:44. Jesus is talking to unbelieving Jews in this passage. They have a *ritual* of religion but don't accept God as their ruler. They are proud, cruel, and cold-blooded. Our Lord says, *"You belong to your father, the Devil, and you want to carry out your father's desire. He was a murderer from the beginning, not holding to the truth, for there is no truth in him. When he lies, he speaks his native language, for he is a liar and the father of lies."*

Nearly every word in this verse alerts us to the character of our Enemy. First of all, he is seen as a "father" of all wicked men. The Greek word for *"devil"* means literally, *"one who leads others into disgrace; to deliberately misrepresent."* Our Enemy is a murderer. There is no truth in him. He is full of dirty tricks.

Note the phrase, *"he speaks his native language . . . ."* He never, ever, under any circumstances, tells the truth. As the "father of lies," his children never hear the truth about anything.

WHAT DOES THE FATHER OF LIES DO TO UNBELIEVERS?

Read 2 Corinthians 4:3-4 to find the answer. Then, 1 John 5:19 tells us how far his evil control has spread: *". . . the whole world is under the control of the evil one."* The whole world is one gigantic prison, and everyone in it is a spiritual prisoner. Satan is the warden of the prison, and he works to darken every mind.

Have you ever played the party game where a person is blindfolded and then told to stand on a wide board? Two people lift the board a couple of inches and wobble it, and then secretly put it down on the floor. The party-goers kneel down and describe how *high* the board is being lifted up! Since their voices are now lower than the victim's head, the illusion is strong. Finally, the blindfolded person is told, "Jump off the board!" Expecting to fall down from a great height, the person is jolted when the "jump" to the floor is about one inch.

I was once the blindfolded person in this game, and it was not pleasant to discover how I was tricked! Thinking back on that event, I realize it was much like the ruse Satan plays on every unbeliever. With blinded minds, people go through life thinking they are soaring to heights of success and future happiness. *What a shock when they discover they have been deceived!*

Satan knows that he and his demons will be cast into the lake of fire (Matthew 25:41). He also knows that all the ungodly will be sent there with him (Revelation 21:8). One of his names means *"the destroyer."* He is determined to keep us as prisoners, to blind us from understanding the truth about God's love for us.

BRINGING UNBELIEVERS TO CHRIST IS WARFARE!

Satan is not going to release any of his captives without a fight. Simply explaining the plan of salvation to one of his prisoners will not be effective. They must be able to see *the Kingdom of God* before they will have a desire to enter it. Satan sends deceiving spirits of error to block the minds of unbelievers. Therefore, we must understand that this is a *spiritual battle.*

> **List below two relatives or friends who are not Christians and who are blind to the reality of God's love:**
>
> **1.** _____
>
> **2.** _____

> **How would you describe their blindness to the gospel? (Check check all that apply:)**
>
> ☐ **They are in total darkness, 100% blind.**
>
> ☐ **My previous attempts to talk about Christ to them have been rudely rebuffed.**
>
> ☐ **There is no comprehension of God or the love of Christ. They are totally deceived.**

How do you feel about your responsibility to help these persons know the Christ Who dwells in you? Have you given them up as "hopeless?" If so, Satan has neutralized the power of God in you. You ask, "But what more can I do?"

Let's return to the principle we learned in Week 6, Day 5 (page 69). In that section, we learned the importance of *"praying until . . ."* Prevailing prayer is *warfare praying.* We shall have much to say about that in the next few days.

HERE'S HOW TO PRAY FOR YOUR FRIEND:

Use your "Listening Room" notebook now. Reserve a blank page for each person. Write the name of the unbeliever on the top line. Next, reflect on all you know about this person. Write down all the *deceptions,* the *evil habits,* the *distorted beliefs,* etc. that you know to be in this person's life. Include the date you recorded all this information. This page becomes your "battle ground" strategy!

Begin to pray *daily* for this person when you go to the "Listening Room." Pray against every stronghold you have listed. Prevail upon the Lord to set the victim free from these bonds. As you observe more deceptions, add them to your pages. In addition, ask the Lord to provide you with openings to *simply serve* this person, to *show love and concern* in every possible way.

Satan is not all-powerful. He has no defense to stop *agape* from penetrating the prison cells! Through the years, I have taught many believers just like you to begin their battle for souls in this simple way. Scores have shared with me the changes which have come because of the power of *"praying until . . ."*

Week 9, Day 3
This Unit: Facing the Powers
This Week: The Battle for Men's Souls
Today: The Power of "Praying Until . . ."

Read Psalm 30:4-5; Psalm 126:5-6; Ezekiel 22:30

A TRUE STORY

Lila and her husband had been working through the principle of "praying until . . ." with me in our cell group. She shared a deep burden with me: "My mother is 72 years old. She used to be one of the most famous movie stars in the Philippines. After I was born, she divorced my father and became hardened toward people. After having our first child, my husband and I became Christians. My mother goes into a rage whenever I try to talk to her about what has happened to us. I have *never* been able to give her my testimony."

Together, we prepared a page for her mother in her "Listening Room" journal (see below). She began to spend daily time "praying until . . ." I shall never forget a lovely weekend when our cell group went to Touch Ranch, near Bellville, Texas, for a retreat. Early one morning, I came out of the house to watch the beautiful sunrise. There, in the semi-darkness, was Lila. "Good morning," I said; "Have you been out here for a long time?"

"I've been out here all night, Ralph," she said. "I feel like my mother's spiritual condition is like a lead weight, crushing my heart." She began to sob as she related her burden. Gently, I read Psalm 126:5-6, and then we prayed together.

🌹 MOTHER

The page from Lila's "Listening Room" journal looked something like this. . .

STARTING DATE I BEGAN TO PRAY	SITUATIONS TO BE PRAYED FOR	DATE PRAYER WAS ANSWERED
February 4	Refusal to speak about Christ	March 12
February 4	Refusal to share her past hurts	March 5
February 4	Rejection of my husband and daughter	March 1
February 4	Refusal to have a Bible in her home	March 15
March 1	That she will receive our love	March 5
March 12	That my sharing will be good seed	March 15
March 15	That she will visit our cell group party	April 1
April 10	That she will agree to hear Ralph preach	April 20
April 20	That her heart will long to know Christ	May 25
May 25	For Mother's growth as a Christian	
May 29	For her desire to join our cell group	

About a month later, I went to the pulpit to preach and saw Lila, her husband and her daughter, sitting in their regular place. Beside her was a gorgeous 72-year-old lady! As my eyes caught Lila's, she nodded "Yes. It's mother!"

For the following month, Lila and her mother shared deeply for the first time in their lives. All the pain of the movie star's past was finally revealed, and Lila was able to talk freely about life in the Kingdom. *I shall never forget the Sunday morning her mother made a public confession of her surrender to the Lordship of Christ.* God's presence had in-vaded the darkness of a woman who had blotted out any thought of Him for decades. It was, in part, the result of a daughter's fervent prayer.

NO ONE TO STAND IN THE GAP?

Ezekiel 22:30 needs a bit of explanation for you to appreciate it. At the time God said these words, Jerusalem was in ruins. It had no defensive wall around it to keep out enemies. Thus, the city symbolizes people who are left without anyone to defend them.

In this Scripture, the enemy God describes are the wicked leaders of Israel, who are leading the people into bondage. He describes their actions in verse 27: *"Her officials within her are like wolves tearing their prey; they shed blood and kill people to make unjust gain."* Jerusalem is compared to people who have no barrier between them and their attackers.

God is the One speaking these words: *"I looked for a man among them who would build up the wall and stand before me in the gap on behalf of the land so I would not have to destroy it, but I found none."*

Through the centuries, including this one, we have received terrible reports of "ethnic cleansing." The holocaust of World War 2 brings pain to all who read about it. Ruthless soldiers killed, tortured, and raped defenseless civilians. In 1993, the world stood back and watched while Bosnian Serbs did the same thing, week after week. Television pictures of the ruthless carnage made the entire world angry — but for weeks and months no one acted to stop it.

Ezekiel 22:30 is talking about those who are in contact with you who are being destroyed by Satan. They have no "protective walls" to stop his terrible attacks. When we, as Kingdom citizens, ignore their terrible plight, the protection God wants them to receive is not provided. *Intercessory prayer for the lost is "standing in the gap."* It is a powerful protector, stopping the freedom of Satan to destroy life without hindrance.

The text says, *"I looked for a man . . . who would . . . stand before me . . . on behalf of . . ."* This is a stirring fact: Many of those who can be brought into the Kingdom are being destroyed because *no Christian cares enough about them to pray for them!*

Your time in the "Listening Room," interceding for unbelievers, links God's mercy to their corrupted minds and hearts. 1 Corinthians 7:13-14 teaches us that *"if a woman has a husband who is not a believer and he is willing to live with her, she must not divorce him. For the unbelieving husband has been sanctified through his wife, and the unbelieving wife has been sanctified through her believing husband."* That word *"sanctified"* means literally, *"being set apart, made holy."* In other words, the Christian who is married to an unbeliever is to "stand in the gap" in intercession.

It is a very serious matter to live around people you know are blinded by Satan and simply ignore their condition. The millions in Cambodia who suffered the "cleansing" of the Khmer Rouge have literally left their bones sticking up out of the ground in the Killing Fields. A friend of mine told of the horror of seeing a leg bone in such a position with his own eyes. *Those bones remind a heartless world that no one came to protect them.*

Living in the Kingdom of God means becoming accountable for what others ignore. Are you ready to *stand in the gap and do battle against the great Destroyer's ruthless ways? It's time once again to go to the "Listening Room."*

Week 9, Day 4
This Unit: Facing the Powers
This Week: The Battle for Men's Souls
Today: What Makes Us Significant?

Read Romans 10:3; 2 Corinthians 4:3-4

From the first day of life, we pattern our actions after the people who are closest to us. As children, we imitate the attitudes and actions of those in our home. Satan knows that, and he launches his plot to destroy us at the time of our birth.

In *Search For Significance*, Robert McGee points out Satan has three lies he will use to destroy us:

1. He wants to misrepresent the character of God.
2. He wants us to believe that God's love is conditional and is based upon our performance.
3. He wants us to look to another person for approval, instead of looking to God for it.

Usually, our parents instilled these three lies in us. They communicated by both words and actions, "Your *significance* depends upon your *performance*. If you want my love, you must perform properly. I will withhold my love when your performance displeases me." For a large percentage of us, receiving "love" from our parents was a sort of *reward* — for eating all the food on our plate, making good grades in our studies, or being successful in some sport. Later on, our parents gave us their approval when we became successful or made a lot of money. We learned very early that if our parents didn't like our *performance*, we'd lose their *"love."* We felt we had no worth.

Satan has developed this pattern in every person who has ever lived. We see it in the very first family. Eve said, "I want to be as significant as God!" Adam said, "Eve, I want to be significant too!" When their two sons were born, they learned from observing their parents that they had to do something important to be significant. When Cain felt he was not as accepted as his brother Abel, he murdered him. It didn't take long for the human race to decide that being *significant* is more important than a human life.

You may be certain of this: *Every unbeliever seeks to be significant through the way he/she performs — and there is at least one other person looked to for approval.* Remember this as you battle for the souls of those you seek to bring into the Kingdom.

Thus, the unbeliever lives in constant fear (see illustration on page 101). Having no significance means having no value, that you are *worthless*. Since Satan's power from the battleground extends directly into the spirit of the unbeliever, he has no knowledge of God's acceptance. He must *achieve* to have worth.

In the kingdoms of this world, there are tens of thousands of choices Satan offers. He asks, "Would you like to be *famous*? Would you like to be *rich*? Would you like to have *degrees* after your name? Would you like to be an *athlete* of great reputation?

How about *owning factories* or being a *great musician?*" He offers lots of choices for those who don't *want* to compete, including the use of drugs or alcohol. It is easy for such persons to find others who want to register their *insignificance*. Together, they form Satan's subcultures: cults, mysticism, gangs or triads, causes to crusade for, political issues to battle about, etc.

The list goes on: He says, "Use your attractive *body* to gain attention and follow the *fashion* trail. Or, busy yourself with *recreation* that becomes your idol rather than your relaxation. Worship at the shrine of the *stock market* or enjoy *gourmet*

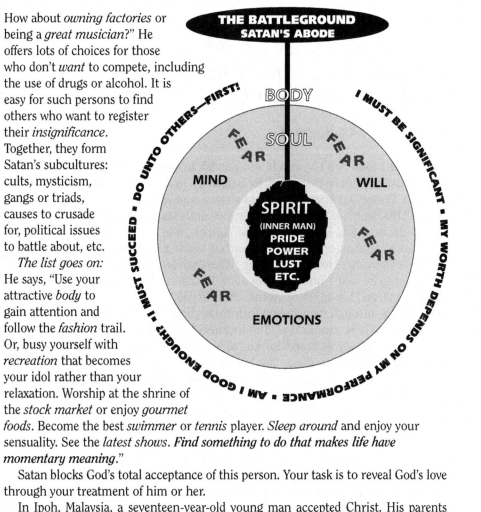

foods. Become the best *swimmer* or *tennis* player. *Sleep around* and enjoy your sensuality. See the *latest shows. Find something to do that makes life have momentary meaning.*"

Satan blocks God's total acceptance of this person. Your task is to reveal God's love through your treatment of him or her.

In Ipoh, Malaysia, a seventeen-year-old young man accepted Christ. His parents worshiped Hanemun, the monkey god. His father, Mr. Cheng, was *furious* when he found out about it. He beat his son and threw him out of the house. That night the lad had no place to go. He decided to sleep on the front steps of his house. In that culture, people remove shoes upon entering the house and store them in a little cupboard on the front porch. Seeing those shoes, the young man got a rag and polished every pair.

The next night, in addition to polishing the shoes he waxed his father's car. For one week he continued to sleep on the porch and serve his angry father in every possible way. It was then that his father began to weep and embraced not only his son but also faith in the Lord Jesus Christ.

What does the Holy Spirit want to do through you to reveal His servant love, His unconditional acceptance of the unbelievers in your life? *Shall we go to the "Listening Room?"*

Week 9, Day 5
This Unit: Facing the Powers
This Week: The Battle for Men's Souls
Today: Containers for Christ

Read Philippians 2:4-8; Acts 20:24

Ruth and I took our 12-year-old son Randall to war-torn Vietnam in January of 1975. We did not remain there long, for Saigon fell in April to the harsh soldiers from the north. During our brief stay, I heard about a man who was simply known as "The Brother." His fame had traveled all the way from the east side of the city to our area miles to the west. Reg Reimer, one of my partners, and I set out to find him.

We parked my beat-up microbus on a street beside a massive slum area. Reg used his perfect Vietnamese to ask a passerby, "Where can we find 'The Brother'?" His eyes brightened as he said, "Turn into this alley. Watch out for the mud. Go about one minute's walk and ask again. Someone will help you."

We slogged through the winding path through wooden and bamboo shacks and kept asking, "Where can we find 'The Brother'?" These destitute slum dwellers all knew him, and slowly we found our way to his house in the heart of the area. It was larger than the one-room shacks but built out of the same materials. We entered to meet "The Brother," who was dressed in the rough cloth worn by rice farmers. He was feeding some half-starved people, doling out plates of rice and fish to them. When he finished, we sat down to visit. He spoke perfect English and French, and had a Ph.D. from the Sorbonne in France.

Formerly a Catholic priest, he had broken with the finery and ritual of the cathedral in the center of the city to live among the poor. He said to me, "Our Lord became a servant to tell us that God loves us without any conditions attached. These people have nothing, so no one cares about them. Christ has put me here to be His heart of love in the middle of this slum."

As we shared, he told us he had spent years translating the book of Psalms from Hebrew into Vietnamese. Tediously, he had made every line a translation that could be sung using the tones of the Vietnamese language. From a dusty book case, he presented me with a printed copy that had little worm holes in it, one of only a dozen or so he still owned.

I was overwhelmed by my encounter with this brilliant man who lived in the center of a rat-infested, diseased community! He explained he held mass every night at eight o'clock and sang the Psalms in Vietnamese, and all were welcome to come. I returned with Ruth several times to attend this service, standing with residents of the area in a circle as he led us in worship. He, in turn, came often on his bicycle to hear me preach at the little church I pastored far to the west.

During our conversations he always turned the topic to Philippians 2:4-8. He said, "We must have the attitude of Christ. He made Himself nothing, and became a Servant. There is no other way to show a ruined world the Father's love!"

Never before, or since, have I known a person who so totally penetrated a

102

community with the knowledge of God's love. Not only were scores and scores of people in that slum kept alive by the food and medicine he procured, but hundreds also came to pray with him and worship the Eternal Father instead of Buddha. He was simply a man committed to revealing Christ.

We had to leave Vietnam as things came to the end. Our missionary companions evacuated a few weeks after we moved to Singapore. We learned from them that the Viet Cong had a list of dangerous people in Saigon who were to be executed at once upon entering the city, including Father Vey.

I have often wondered how "The Brother" came to his end. Was it by torture or beheading, or a single shot through that brilliant brain? Was he standing in the candle-lit bamboo chapel where we worshiped with him when the soldiers broke in and took his life? Was he singing one of his lovely psalms as he died?

HE IS NO FOOL WHO GIVES WHAT HE CANNOT KEEP TO GAIN WHAT HE CANNOT LOSE

One day in heaven I will meet him, and neither one of us will care how his life ended. He had actually *died* long before his murder. He had died to self, to ambition, to personal reputation. He had been living in the fellowship and presence of the indwelling Christ for years. Like Paul, he was able to say, *"However, I consider my life worth nothing to me, if only I may finish the race and complete the task the Lord Jesus has given me — the task of testifying to the gospel of God's grace" (Acts 20:24).*

Whenever the Master causes me to recall "The Brother," I pray, "Lord, I want you to shape my heart to be like his. You may not assign me to live in a slum, but let my heart be ready for whatever assignment you give to me." Would you pray that prayer with me? The *PAIS* of the Kingdom, sooner or later, must make a deliberate choice to follow his/her Lord without reservation.

Do you still remember these words from Week 7, Day 4 (page 81)?

It is the task of a servant to obey his Master.

**It is the obligation of the Master
to provide for that servant.**

**Therefore, the servant need
never be afraid!**

Week 10, Day 1
This Unit: Facing the Powers
This Week: The Wrestling Match
Today: Principalities

Read Ephesians 1:20-21, 6:10-18; Romans 8:38-39

In Ephesians 1, heaven is described, where Christ is seated at the right hand of the Father. We are told in Ephesians 2:6 that we are also seated there. Paul then discusses those who occupy the *battleground*, and reminds us that Christ is greater than those who live there. (Refer to illustration on page 20.)

In Ephesians 1:21, who does Paul describe as living in the battleground?

☐ All rulers.

☐ All authorities.

☐ All power.

☐ All dominion (territories).

☐ Every title that can be given.

☐ All of the above.

In these passages, he sets the scene for teaching about the events that transpire in heaven, on the battleground and on the earth. When we come to Ephesians 6, humans are described as living in the *heavenly realms*. We are told we are in a "struggle" — literally, a "wrestling match." He then describes our opponents.

In Ephesians 6:12, who does Paul describe as living in the battleground?

☐ Rulers.

☐ Authorities.

☐ Powers of this dark world.

☐ Spiritual forces of evil in the heavenly realms.

☐ All of the above.

Compare the two lists. It is obvious that when we are seated with Christ in *heaven*, these opponents are *below* us on the *battleground*. Since Christ *lives in us*, we need never be under their power and control.

In Ephesians 6:13, when do we wrestle with these spiritual forces?

_____

_____

This term describes periods of time when anguish and hurt attack us. The sources are not from the world around us, but from the spiritual forces of evil on the battleground. A condition of poverty and pain is defined. As we live in the Kingdom of God on the earth, we may expect attacks from the "spiritual forces of evil" from the battleground. Who are these enemies? An examination of the terms will help us understand them.

Rulers: Those who are first in political rank or power.
Authorities: Those having the power to use force on others.
Powers of this dark world: World rulers.
Spiritual forces of evil in the heavenly realms: A group of hurtful creatures.

In addition to these supernatural creatures, Satan is described in verse 16 as "the evil one." He directs these invisible powers who have clearly defined levels of authority. They are the "flaming arrows" he throws at us, bringing anguish and hurt.

Notice that *you are not set free from these powers when you become a Christian.* That's why Paul tells us to wear the "full armor of God." If you are wearing it, you will "be able to stand your ground" and after you have "done everything," you will stand in victory.

THE BAD NEWS AND THE GOOD NEWS

Scripture never promises that living in the Kingdom will be painless. Peter wrote, *"Dear friends, do not be surprised at the painful trial you are suffering, as though something strange were happening to you. But rejoice that you participate in the sufferings of Christ, so that you may be overjoyed when his glory is revealed"* (1 Peter 4:12-13). That's the *bad* news.

The *good* news is that Satan and his spiritual forces are under the power of heaven, and we are under the protective care of the Holy Spirit.

 In the scripture below, <u>underline</u> every condition mentioned that might be powerful enough to separate us from God's love:

> *"For I am convinced that neither death nor life, neither angels nor demons, neither the present nor the future, nor any powers, neither height nor depth, nor anything else in all creation, will be able to separate us from the love of God that is in Christ Jesus our Lord."* **(Romans 8:38-39)**

Recognize these important truths:
1. We are seated with Christ in heaven, yet live on the earth.
2. There are spiritual forces on the battleground, seeking to attack and destroy us.
3. Ephesians 6:13 refers to a time called "the day of evil," when without warning Satan's forces will attack us.
4. Since we never know when that will take place, we are *always to be prepared.*
5. We have received protective garments and weapons of warfare, which ensure that we can stand when the attacks come.

After this introduction, we will spend the rest of this unit getting acquainted with our armor and weapons. These are everyday garments, not just put on at special times!

Week 10, Day 2
This Unit: Facing the Powers
This Week: The Wrestling Match
Today: Onward, Christian Soldiers!

Read Ephesians 3:10-11

Like sentries at their guard posts, we must always stand in readiness for spiritual combat. We must recognize that demonic enemies are behind much of what comes against us to hurt us. As you leave the "Listening Room" each day, consciously put on the spiritual armor God supplies. Be ready for battle. It's important for us to wear our body armor, but there is something much more significant to consider first of all.

BATTLES ARE WON BY ARMIES, NOT BY SINGLE SOLDIERS
Read slowly through Ephesians 6:10-18. You will discover that Paul is writing to a collective group, not to individuals. The pro-nouns "you", "your", or "we" are *always in the plural*. It is ridiculous to think of one soldier marching alone into a battlefield, isn't it? Like any other battle, spiritual warfare is a task best faced by a group.

Think of the logistics required to fight a war. Soldiers train *together*, not separately. Whether it is climbing steep trails or digging trenches, they are always organized to be part of a group. Look back at the listings of Satan's forces on page 104. Every reference is in the plural. *God's forces are also organized to enter into battle by groups!*

 Thoughtfully read Ephesians 3:10-11 below. <u>Underline</u> the single word which explains the way God reveals his wisdom to Satan's forces:

"His intent was that now, through the church, the manifold wisdom of God should be made known to the rulers and authorities in the Heavenly realms, according to His eternal purpose which He accomplished in Christ Jesus our Lord."

Did you recognize the *plurality* of the word you underlined? Your life in Christ makes participation in your cell group the highest priority of Kingdom life. Let's expand our thinking about how the *"manifold* wisdom of God" is going to be made known to Satan's thugs. The word *"manifold"* isn't a common word. It is important to understand what it means. It means "many colored." (Think of Joseph's coat as *"manifold,"* for it had many colors.)

WHO ATTENDS YOUR CELL GROUP?
Of course, you can name each *person* who attends, but don't stop there! Is the Holy Spirit present? Of course — and your time of worship celebrates that fact. Afterwards, you begin to *edify (oikodomeo)* one another. A strong spiritual insight flows from the Father to your heart, and you share it as an encouragement to a cell member who is struggling. A sister reads a psalm which has a powerful truth for the group. You gather around a

member who suffers from bone cancer. As you lay hands on the person and pray together, a sense that God is healing comes to the group. There follows a session with one of the members who quietly says, "I came to the cell group tonight to confess my sin. I have grieved the Lord and I have injured this body by my critical spirit. Please pray that I will yield this matter fully to my Master, and hold me accountable for what I share."

WHO ELSE IS PRESENT?

Are there any spirit beings gathered with you? Psalm 91:11 says, *"For he will command his angels concerning you to guard you in all your ways."* And, read this comment by the writer of Hebrews: *". . . You have come to thousands upon thousands of angels in joyful assembly, to the church of the firstborn, whose names are written in heaven . . . ."* (12:22-23). Since they don't need chairs, they can really pack in around you!

LAST, BUT NOT LEAST . . .

Don't think for a split second that Satan will allow a gathering of the citizens of the Kingdom and not be represented! You have **spiritual forces of evil** present in your gathering. They have come to represent their boss, who goes about like a roaring lion, seeking armorless Christians to devour. They are there in a plurality: the *"rulers and authorities in the heavenly realms."* Just give these evil forces a foothold, and they will deceive you.

But something is happening which is very special. An *"eternal purpose"* is about to take place. As the presence of the Holy Spirit causes His gifts to flow, the "many colored" wisdom of God is being made known to the rulers and authorities who came from the second heaven to attend your cell group. You see, your spiritual gifts are like a rainbow in the sky, a promise that God will preserve His children. The demonic creatures who came to harm cry out in pain as blinding light pierces their darkness.

If you have attended your cell group for very long, I am certain you have experienced what I have experienced for many years. Somewhere towards the end of the session, there's a sense of lightness, of relief, of joy felt by all. Most of the time, our cell meeting ends with hugs being shared all around. I can't count the times I have helped Ruthie clean up the cups and things left behind, singing a praise song out loud.

That's what happens when the principalities flee from what the Father accomplished in us through Christ Jesus. The group really never got around to addressing demons and squirming because we felt attacked by them. They simply fled because we were being the "called out ones," the church!

My visit to the church in Abidjan, Ivory Coast was unforgettable. There are more than 30,000 people in their cell groups, and at Easter time they gathered with unbelievers they invited and brought to a special time of worship and preaching. Pastor Dion Robert stood quietly on the platform and said, "Now, we are going to pray and invite the Holy Spirit to come. If you need a special touch from Him, ask Him for it. If you need healing, don't come forward. He will heal you in your seat. Just ask Him." After a minute or so of dead silence, some began to praise the Lord for what He was doing in their lives. Simultaneously, many who had been dedicated to demons while still in their mother's wombs, began to cry out in pain and writhe on the ground. They were lovingly carried away for ministry and deliverance. I literally watched demons flee!

May God help you see this truth. It's life-changing. Battles are fought by armies, and your cell group is a squad!

Week 10, Day 3
This Unit: Facing the Powers
This Week: The Wrestling Match
Today: Marching As to War

Read Ephesians 6:10-18

GOD'S ARMOR IS FOR OUR PROTECTION

In Ephesians 6:14-17, Paul describes the combat dress of a first-century Roman soldier. The soldier put on his armor *before* entering battle. Since the enemies we face are evil spiritual beings, the armor we wear must be spiritual. In Romans 13:12, Paul calls it *"the armor of light."* God gives us the armor! Therefore, our enemy has no access to it. *Not one* of these items can be found in Satan's weaponry. Further-more, Satan has *no weapons* to pierce our protection. We are safe!

> In Ephesians 6:14-17, where are these pieces of armor to be placed? (Draw lines from the items in the left column to the parts of the body protected by them in the right column:)

Belt of truth	**Feet**
Breastplate of righteousness	**Head**
Gospel of peace	**Back**
Shield of faith	**Waist**
Helmet of salvation	**Arm/hand**
	Chest

Aha! You found one part of the body without any armor provided, didn't you? The reason the *back* has no protection is that we are never to turn our backs on our enemy. Ephesians 6:18 says, *"Be alert."* Facing the principalities, we take the territory purchased by the blood of Christ on the cross. When He cried *"It is finished"* *(John 19:30)*, it was a guarantee that our victory is assured. Abraham Kuyper wrote, "There is no sphere of life over which Christ does not say, *'That's mine!'*"

Look over the list again. Is not Christ Himself the armor we wear? Did He not say, "I am the *Truth*"? He alone is our *Righteousness*. He alone is our *Peace*, "Who has broken down every wall." He is our Source of continual *salvation*. We place in front of us our *faith* in the Son of God (Galatians 2:20). Our protection will never be penetrated. The One Who sends us into battle is Himself our protection.

In Luke 10, we see Jesus sending out his disciples two-by-two. They are going to engage in warfare. *The ultimate goal of all spiritual warfare is to bring the lost to Jesus*. Therefore, He sent them to declare that the Kingdom of God had come to an area called Perea (modern day Jordan). It's interesting that He said, "I am sending you out like lambs among wolves" (verse 3). Did you know that sheep have no means of self-protection? They have no fangs, no claws — nothing! *Whew! That's scary!*

Scary? Not really. You see, they know their shepherd will protect them. We, too, must enter the conflict knowing He is not only in us, but is *protecting* us. He is in us and He is our armor. He has promised He will never leave or forsake us.

OUR WEAPONS ARE FOR DEMOLITION

Our chief weapon in the encounter with Satan's army is *"the sword of the Spirit, which is the word of God."* While this obviously is referring to every chapter in the Bible, the *written* Word of God, it must be seen as including the *illumination* given to us by the Holy Spirit about specific situations. A military officer studies manuals that explain warfare tactics, but when he is in the middle of a battle, he makes decisions based not only on the manuals but also on the orders given by his commander.

The same thing applies to spiritual warfare. As we enter the domain of Satan's kingdoms to rescue unbelievers and bring them to Christ, we must be sensitive to *all* God says to us, both through Scripture and through words coming directly from the Holy Spirit. The power of the word of God is awesome!

I am thinking of a university student I was seeking to bring to Christ. He said, "Don't talk to me about the Bible! I don't believe in it." *Of course he didn't!* His mind was blinded by Satan's deceptions. What he didn't understand was that the *word of God* has power whether he believed in it or not. I had no intention of laying aside Scripture as I talked. As I recited John 3:16 to him, he was being stirred by the Holy Spirit. He said, "I find it hard to believe that God *loves*. If he is so powerful, why should he care about humanity?" *He was searching for truth! He was starting to ask questions.* That meant some light was dawning in his dark soul. I could sense Satan's demonic powers screaming in pain. Quoting Scripture after Scripture, hour after hour, I finally helped him pray to receive Christ. The very Word of God he *"didn't believe in"* was like a sword that penetrated his darkness.

Let's begin to practice Paul's assignment for us to *"pray in the Spirit on all occasions with all kinds of prayers and requests."* Praying in the Spirit is not a weapon. It is the *activity* of the battle itself. The armor and the sword must be present, but the battle involves prayer. The "Listening Room" emerges once again in our *Arrival Kit* journey as crucial to the work of the Kingdom of God. In your Bible, underline this phrase in Ephesians 6:18: *". . . always keep on praying for all the saints."*

What does it mean to *"pray in the Spirit?"* I am sure you already know how to pray when you are *not* in the Spirit. It can be a dry, ritualistic routine that leaves you bored or tired, but when you pray knowing there is a war going on, it's not the same. "Standing in the gap" (see page 99) is praying in the Spirit. Do not be surprised when God bestows spiritual gifts to make such praying more powerful. *Visit the "Listening Room" now!*

Week 10, Day 4
This Unit: Facing the Powers
This Week: The Wrestling Match
Today: Three Levels of Warfare

Read 2 Corinthians 10:3-5; Matthew 16:18-19

Today's Scriptures make it clear that our warfare is not of this world, and the weapons we use are all supernatural. 2 Cor. 10:3-5, 9 has some interesting Greek words. You might like to write a note about them in the margin of your Bible.

In verse 4, the word *"strongholds"* means *"fortresses,"* like a castle built with a thick wall to stop all invaders. God's power in us is a weapon that can destroy these demonic barriers.

In verse 5, the word for *"arguments"* refers to *"imaginations"* or *"speculations."* It is connected to the thought life of a person. The word *"pretension"* in the New International Version, is *"high tower"* in the Greek. One scholar says it refers to the ancient tower of Babel, where men decided they would build a tower that would reach all the way to heaven.

The Kingdom of God on the earth today dwells within us, and we live in a constant battleground. It's interesting that when Jesus first mentioned the church in Matthew 16:18-19, He located it right up against *"the gates of hell,"* and promised we would never lose the battles fought there, binding and loosing on earth what has already been bound and loosed in heaven. We are the victors!

In *Warfare Prayer,** Dr. Peter Wagner describes three general levels of our spiritual warfare:

1. Ground-level spiritual warfare. This is the ministry of casting out demons. In Singapore, it is common to deal with those suffering from this problem. Only believers have the authority and power to release people from this form of oppression. Jesus made it clear that deliverance was to be a continuing ministry function of the Body of Christ. Do not think that demonic possession only occurs in Hollywood movies. In Houston, Texas, in the company of a Christian psychiatrist, I ministered for the first time to a woman who was demon possessed. The psychiatrist fully recognized the distinction between emotional hysteria and spiritual problems and brought the woman to me for deliverance.

2. Occult-level spiritual warfare. All over this world, without exception, Satan has implanted the occult as a prison cell around thousands of persons. In Africa, women drink the blood of a goat to become pregnant and then teach their children to worship a demon. In Brazil, I have seen those who have had a leg amputated by their parents as a sacrifice to a demon. In Singapore, I have seen the possessed who have been given the blood of a Taoist priest to drink.

In America, I have worked with people brainwashed by the Unification Church or New Age channelers. While I was teaching in a Christian school, a student from South Carolina (a "Bible-belt" state!) asked me for help. He had been making animal

---

* Peter Wagner's book, *Warfare Prayer*, is published by Regal Books in the United States and Monarch Publications, Ltd., in England.

sacrifices to Satan since he was 14 years old. As you minister in the Kingdom of God, your cell group will, from time to time, confront both of these levels of warfare. If you are a "soldier" without battle experience, seek help from those in the ministry of your church — but don't run away from such persons. They desperately need to be set free.

3. Strategic-level spiritual warfare. This is Wagner's term for recognizing we need to pray against "territorial spirits." Paul was talking about this when he wrote, *"For our struggle is not against flesh and blood, but against the rulers, against the authorities, against the powers of this dark world and against the spiritual forces of evil in the heavenly realms."*

On page 24, we examined Daniel 10:12-13 as one example of the battles that occur in the second heaven. "Principalities and powers" refer to evil spiritual beings who control geographical areas, groups of people, or particular sins. Their domination over certain areas is obvious to the sensitive Christian.

For example, in Singapore the Chinese word *"Kiasu"* is commonly used to refer to the "spirit" of the population. There is even a comic strip by that name. The word means, "Altogether everything I want for myself!" This is a very evil desire, based on self-glorification. *As we prayed for the country, it was revealed to us that the specific principality over the nation is named "Kiasu."*

Amsterdam is a city that displays 5,000 prostitutes in store windows. Bangkok has many times that number and most of them are girls sold by their own parents when they reach adolescence. What do these cities have in common? *The specific principality over them is Prostitution.*

In the United States, one quickly realizes that principalities reign over different territories. In San Francisco it is Homosexuality, in New Orleans it is Orgies, in Washington, D.C., it is Power.

What can be done? Roger Forster and his associates in London have organized "Jesus Marches" to declare to the principalities that Christ has come to take possession of Satan's territories. Here in Singapore, the cell groups have half-nights of prayer, sometimes walking quietly through housing estates and praying against the principalities present there. One can go into any district of a city and sense the demonic power that rules over it.

Your cell group needs to be in a spirit of prayer at all of these three levels. Meeting as a group to pray over your lists of strongholds in the lives of unbelievers is an important task *(see page 99).* Walking or driving through a neighborhood together and praying for the unreached residents will bear spiritual fruit.

Remember that our individual blind spots and vices are usually common to the culture around us. That culture is penetrated deeply by principalities and powers. Dealing with this matter is one of the toughest things for a Christian to do. There is a Chinese saying, *"Never ask a fish what water is like."* For that reason, the voices of spiritual prophets are as important today as they were in Israel of old.

What do *you* do to gain personal significance? Who are the people *you* are trying to impress? So much of what we wear, where we live, what we drive, how we work, is penetrated by the influence of the principalities and powers around us. You and I will *never change* unless we realize that much of what we are and do is the result of principalities of the air.

Take all these thoughts to the "Listening Room." What do you hear there?

Week 10, Day 5
This Unit: Facing the Powers
This Week: The Wrestling Match
Today: Going on Before

Read Colossians 2:15; 1 Peter 3:22

When I was a teenager, Nate Saint came to Baer Field near Fort Wayne, Indiana and attended our church. He owned a two-seat Piper Cub and taught me to fly. I saw him break up with the most beautiful girl in our church because he sensed she was not called to serve as the wife of a missionary pilot.

When I went to college, I met Jim Elliott and Ed McCulley. Jim was absolutely the most Spirit-filled guy I had ever met, and he left a permanent impression on me when he graduated. I remembered Ed from his ability as a football player and because he was about the only student who drove around in a brand-new automobile. Nate Saint also appeared at that time, finished with his stint in the air force.

Along with Pete Fleming and Roger Youderian, these men went to Ecuador to evangelize the Auca Indian tribe. These head-hunters had never been exposed to the Gospel, and no foreigner had ever survived in their midst.

After many flights over the Auca's jungle area, flights of lowering gifts in a bucket, the men finally landed on the sandy beach of the Curaray River. As they approached the Aucas with love and gifts of friendship, they were hacked to death by machetes. Their bodies were thrown in the river to be eaten by Piranha fish, and precious young wives became widows.

At that time, I was pastoring a small church outside Washington, D.C. I was driving home from making a hospital call when a news bulletin came over my radio. I pulled to the side of the road stunned, and wept and wept.

Upon reaching the house, I found Ruth weeping. We had double dated with Nate and Marge prior to our marriages, and the whole thing seemed so unreal to us.

Because of this traumatic event, our lives were changed forever. Until that point, I was enjoying a ministry that had included a few years working for Billy Graham and planting a church in a fashionable suburb. God had called both of us to serve Him on the mission field, and I had closed my mind to His assignment.

As we prepared ourselves for the mission field, the widows of these fine men determined they would finish the job of reaching the Aucas. Taking a little golden-haired daughter with them, two of the women entered the territory and lived among the men who had murdered their husbands. They remained until the entire tribe had been evangelized. Elizabeth Elliott brought the very man who killed Jim to the United States to tell of the grace that brought him to the Kingdom of God.

Jim Elliott autographed my class yearbook before we left college. By his smiling picture, he wrote: *"He is no fool who gives what he cannot keep to gain what he cannot lose."* Do you know that the word for "witness" in Greek is the source of the English word *"martyr"*? As we face the powers with our *witness*, we must realize it can be a costly matter. The Kingdom of God has many martyrs as well as many witnesses.

As we near the completion of our journey together, you must make a decision about life in the Kingdom. There is really no place for you to "dig in your heels" and say, "This is as far as I go!" The journey has no stopping point. It continues right on into eternity.

As you view the picture shown below, read 1 Corinthians 2:6-9

"And having disarmed the powers and authorities, he made a public spectacle of them, triumphing over them by the cross." (Colossians 2:15).

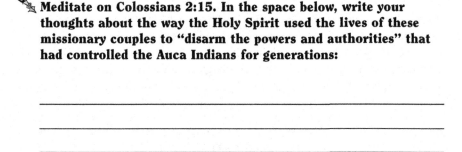 **Meditate on Colossians 2:15. In the space below, write your thoughts about the way the Holy Spirit used the lives of these missionary couples to "disarm the powers and authorities" that had controlled the Auca Indians for generations:**

_____

_____

_____

God guarantees that those who live in His Kingdom do not need to fear death. When Jesus was crucified, Satan thought he had won the battle. Little did he realize how he had been defeated! Death has no sting for us. The joy of our life on earth is the anticipation of what lies ahead. For the unbeliever, death is a tragedy; for us, *"to die is gain"* (Philippians 1:21). One of the toughest paradigms to get rid of is the fear of death. For us, death has no sting and the grave has no victory over us (1 Corinthians 15:55).

1 Peter 3:22 is another one of the many verses you might wish to underline in your Bible. It reminds us that Christ *"has gone into heaven and is at God's right hand — with angels, authorities and powers in submission to him."* The five men who were martyred in Ecuador are now celebrating the final skirmish which brought the Aucas to Christ. They are seated with Christ in heaven. Soon we will be there, too!

Week 11, Day 1
This Week: The Journey Beyond
Today: You Are a Minister

Read 1 Corinthians 12:1-12; Acts 2:44-47; Ephesians 4:7-16, 29, 32

A grandmother used to tell the story of her four-year-old grandson, whose father was a pastor. One day she asked the little boy, "What do you want to be when you grow up?" He answered, "I'm gonna be a 'peecher' (preacher) like my Dad. Gramma, I'm a 'peecher' now, but I just can't 'peech'!"

> **Is that the way you think about your being called to be a "minister"?**
>
> **What images come to mind when you hear the word minister?**
>
> **Write them below:** _____
>
> _____
>
> _____
>
> _____
>
> _____

Most of the time, the leaders in the church are called "pastors." These people are traditionally seen as *the* ministers and even given a special title, "clergy." Around the world, the Holy Spirit is helping Christians break through Satan's deception that the church is made up of a special "clergy" and the rest of the people who are called the "laity." In ministry, there should be no division between the "clergy" and the "laity," even though this division has existed for centuries within the church. Satan inserted the clergy-laity division into church life very slowly. It took almost 300 years for him to strangle the original lifestyle of the Bride of Christ, the Church. By accomplishing his objective, he crippled the church's ministry.

In the first few weeks of the church, there were more than 3,000 believers who met to hear the apostles teach in the temple courts. The apostles' ministry took place as they moved from house to house to build up fellow Christians, sharing an intimate fellowship meal, and praying for one another. Thus, the disciples of Jesus focused on preparing God's people for works of service, and leading every believer to perform the *actual ministry*.

Through the centuries, no one bothered to examine what was happening to the church. In the time of Martin Luther (A.D. 1517), groups began to be formed which rejected the clergy-laity distinctions. These people were considered so dangerous that some were burned at the stake, some were imprisoned, and some fled to other nations.

Clearly the Bible teaches that God calls leaders in the church. In Ephesians 4:11-12 we are told, *"It was he who gave some to be apostles, some to be prophets, some to be evangelists, and some to be pastors and teachers, to prepare God's people for works of service, so that the body of Christ may be built up . . . "* These leaders are not to be set apart as special people who do all the ministry. This world waits in such desperate need, it cannot be reserved for a privileged few. Instead leaders are to prepare every believer for works of service. God has given them to the church to equip people for ministry, serving as coaches to those in the church.

John Wesley, the founder of the Methodist Church, was one such equipping leader. He was a dynamic preacher, but he realized that the work of God would not go forward unless he prepared every believer to minister to others. Therefore, he organized his people into cell groups called "class meetings," and they became powerful points of ministry that spread throughout England.

In your cell group, you have seen the many ways that God can minister through the different cell members. This is what Paul is talking about in 1 Corinthians 12:4-6 when he writes: *"There are different kinds of gifts, but the same Spirit. There are different kinds of service, but the same Lord. There are different kinds of working, but the same God works all of the in all men."*

> **Read 1 Corinthians 12:7-11 again and think about your cell group. Which of those gifts have you seen in your cell group?**

_____

_____

_____

> **What special ways has God used you to minister to other people?**
> ☐ **Share your testimony**
> ☐ **Encourage a discouraged friend**
> ☐ **Service**
> ☐ **Hospitality**
> ☐ **Believing that God will do the impossible**
> ☐ **Others:**_____

_____

_____

_____

Being used by God to touch a need in another's life is a special honor. It will cause you to spring out of bed every morning with the hope that God can use you each day. It will give you are reason to live that is much bigger than making money, buying a bigger home or getting the kids to baseball practice. You have a gift from God to give to someone else, the gift of life.

Take some time right now to thank our Lord for how he has moved in your cell group. Thank Him for how He has used you to bless other people. Commit your life 100% to Him and tell Him that you will do whatever He asks you to do in service to others.

Week 11, Day 2
This Week: The Journey Beyond
Today: You Are a Priest

Read Revelation 1:6; 1 Peter 2:5, 9, 10; 2 Corinthians 5:11-20

You are a minister! As God's minister, you are also a representative. In the business world, front-line employees like cashiers, waiters, waitresses, and receptionists represent their company. One of their main roles is to project a positive, pleasing image for their employer, their boss. As a Christian, you are God's representative! Your actions and attitudes reflect on your heavenly boss.

The biblical image of the priest is one way to think of the way you represent God in this world. There are a series of verses in the Bible that describe you as a priest. For example, Revelation 1:6 tells us Jesus ". . . *has made us to be a kingdom and priests to serve his God and Father.*" Add the title *"priest"* to *PAIS*. You are a *child*, a *servant*, and a *priest* of God.

A priest is someone who represents God to people and people to God. Peter was speaking of you when he wrote: *"you also, like living stones, are being built into a spiritual house to be a holy priesthood, offering spiritual sacrifices acceptable to God through Jesus Christ. . . . But you are a chosen people, a royal priesthood, a holy nation, a people belonging to God, that you may declare the praises of him who called you out of darkness into his wonderful light. Once you were not a people, but now you are the people of God; once you had not received mercy, but now you have received mercy"* (1 Peter 2:5, 9, 10).

> You are a C_____ people, a R_____
>
> P_____, a holy N_____, a P_____
>
> belonging to G_____.

> According to this passage, why has God called us to be his royal priesthood?
>
> ☐ To experience the fullness of walking in His light but keeping silent about it.
>
> ☐ To share this message with family members only.
>
> ☐ To declare to others how God has brought us out of darkness.

Of course you are to fully experience the fullness of His light and you are to share your faith with your family members. A priest is called to share with others what the Father has done.

Since a priest must be in touch with the Father, he or she must be *holy*. Our righteousness is not the result of keeping commandments. Instead, Christ comes to dwell in us and becomes our righteousness, and we are holy. Then, when he or she ministers, he or she is a *royal* priest and wears the garments belonging to the King's family.

You are a priest. This means you will constantly serve as a go-between, bringing God to people and people to God. An old cowboy in West Texas once spoke to a group of pastors in my presence. He said, "Men, if God has called you to be his servant, never stoop so low as to want to become a king or a president!" What can we possibly accomplish that will have greater value in eternity than to touch God with one hand and lift up fallen people with the other, manifesting His spiritual gifts?

Paul uses the work ambassador as another way of explaining our ministry as a priest and representative. He writes in 2 Corinthians 5:19, "We are therefore Christ's ambassadors, as though God were making his appeal through us. We implore you on Christ's behalf: Be reconciled to God." As an ambassador, we go for god, but it is as if God is doing it through us. We are extensions of God work in the world, acting on His behalf for other people.

In what ways have you seen others in your church or your cell group act as a priest or ambassador to hurting people in the world?

☐ **Praying for the lost**

☐ **Befriending people who need God**

☐ **Inviting unbelievers to dinner**

☐ **Sharing Jesus' love**

☐ **Other**_____

How has God used you to touch people who do not know the Lord?

_____

_____

_____

Spend time in the "Listening Room" as you consider the way you currently represent God and the way you would like to do so. What changes do you need to make?

_____

_____

_____

_____

_____

Week 11, Day 3
This Week: The Journey Beyond
Today: Equipped to Minister

Read 2 Timothy 2:15; Hebrews 13:20-21; 2 Timothy 3:16-17

WHAT YOU NEED

As a minister you need to be prepared; you need to be equipped to serve. The words contained in 2 Timothy 2:15 can be paraphrased: *"With all speed, eagerly present yourself to God as one who is qualified, a hard worker who is not embarrassed by lack of skill, and who knows how to use the word of truth."*

Being equipped to serve effectively is important to your life in God's Kingdom. We have already discovered that your cell group is part of the army of God. Those entering the army are first sent for basic training.

For a few years, I taught in a seminary in a small town that had a basic training school for newly enlisted army personnel. Frequently I would board the airplane in Atlanta to fly home, and there would be only one or two civilians on board. The rest of the passengers were young men and women going to "Boot Camp." Some were a mess, having long hair, scrawny beards, and smelly clothes.

When flying *away* from that town, the plane would once again be full of army personnel. This time, the young men and women were being transferred to another location after their months of training. What a contrast! Neatly pressed uniforms, short hair, and a dignity of bearing made them most impressive. It was hard to believe they were the same people.

When soldiers go into battle, they need to be certain that the soldier standing on either side of them can be depended upon to function effectively. When soldiers' lives are in danger, they need to be able to trust the troops around them!

For this reason you should make a clear commitment to your Lord: *"With all speed, eagerly present yourself to God as one who is qualified..."* Being equipped for ministry is a very serious matter. It requires an investment. God is already doing His part.

Take a moment to review Hebrews 13:20-21.

Who is the ultimate source of your preparation and equipping?

☐ **Your cell leader**
☐ **Your pastor**
☐ **Your mentor**
☐ **The Lord Jesus**

Of course it is the Lord Jesus, "the great Shepherd of the sheep." You are one of His sheep and he has a plan to continue to equip you for "everything good for doing his will." He will use your cell leader, your pastor, your mentor and other people to stimulate your preparation, but He is the final source of every good work.

WHAT YOU CAN EXPECT

As you commit to be equipped, you can expect two things to happen. First, you will grow. You have already begun a journey of spiritual growth by starting and completing *The Arrival Kit*. You've probably noticed changes in your thought processes and your actions. You are becoming more like Christ. Your growth can and should continue. But the completion of *The Arrival Kit* is only one stage of the journey. As you continue to grow, you will learn more about spiritual gifts, evangelism, and leadership. You will see the need for further equipping in these three areas.

Second, Satan will do all he can to thwart your commitment to grow. Be aware of his multiple ways to deceive and discourage. You do not have to yield to his temptation to stagnate. YOU CAN GROW!

Read 2 Timothy 3:16-17 to discover one way to ensure your continued growth.

What does this passage say about your spiritual growth?

_____

_____

_____

_____

Have you committed to a daily routine of reading, understanding, and applying God's word? Go to the "Listening Room," asking God to reveal your heart, your true motives.

After years of ministry all across Asia Minor, Paul was arrested in Jerusalem and taken by ship to Rome to stand trial for his faith. He was very close to the day of his execution, and he remembered the past as he anticipated the eternal future he was about to enter. Under house arrest, he wrote to Timothy, his son in the faith. There are two passages for us to meditate on:

In 2 Timothy 2:11-13, Paul connects actions with consequences. Complete the missing words, evaluating your own situation:

If we D_____ with Him, we will also L_____ with Him.

If we E_____, we will also R_____ with Him.

If we D_____ Him, He will also D_____ us.

If we are F_____, He will remain F_____, for He cannot disown Himself.

119

Week 11, Day 4
This Week: The Journey Beyond
Today: Becoming a Mentor

Read Romans 15:14; 2 Timothy 2:1-2

"I myself am convinced, my brothers, that you yourselves are full of goodness, complete in knowledge and competent to instruct one another." (Romans 15:14)

The verse above shows that you are able to help another Christian grow. One of the ways you can do that is through a mentoring others. Because we cannot grow without assistance from others, your church has developed a one-to-one relationship between cell group members, called the *"mentor-protégé relationship."*

A "protégé" is a person who is guided by a fellow cell group member on the journey into ministry. A "mentor" is a person who takes responsibility for encouraging and helping another cell group member, serving as a guide. Everyone who *is* a mentor *should have* a mentor.

Upon entering your cell group, you became a protégé. As you have journeyed through *The Arrival Kit*, you have met with your mentor on a regular basis. Now that you are completing this material, you will benefit by becoming a mentor and helping someone else go through it. Thus, you will be connected to others in a living chain of love and ministry.

Every Christian should set a goal to become both a protégé and a mentor, functioning in both roles at the same time. In this way, each person is both receiving and giving. Your cell group leader will help you link up with someone else to serve as a mentor. It is a great privilege for you to accept this ministry.

YOU WILL GROW BY BEING A MENTOR

Becoming a mentor is important for your spiritual growth. In order for you to mature as a Christian, you must learn to give of yourself after having benefited from the care of others. In addition, mentoring is vital to cell life, which is sustained by the relationships built between its members. Mentoring ensures there will be automatic follow-up when a member is absent, in need, or falling away from the faith.

When you find yourself in need of assistance in ministering to your protégé, you will find your own mentor at your side, helping you in your ministry.

BEING A MENTOR DOES NOT REQUIRE YOU TO TEACH

Relationship building is the primary task of a mentor. You do not have to be an instructor — only a concerned friend. There should be regular contact between a mentor and his or her protégé. This should take place outside of cell meeting time. Choose a time and place most convenient for both of you. Keep in touch by telephone as needed.

SUGGESTIONS FOR THE MENTOR-PROTÉGÉ RELATIONSHIP

1. Uphold each other in prayer and in cell and celebration attendance.
2. Help each other to spend time in your "Listening Rooms."
3. Encourage your protégé to continue the discipleship process.
4. Help each other by befriending your unsaved friends together.
5. Seek to win at least one person to Christ every six months. Spend time praying for unbelievers in your families and among your friends, always remembering that the most important task of a believer is to bring the lost to the Savior.

FUNCTION AS LINKS IN YOUR GROUP'S PRAYER CHAIN

Mentors and protégés are linked by the cell's prayer chain to all the other members of the group. As concerns or needs surface, share them through the prayer chain.

There will be times when an emergency happens in the life of a cell group member. One telephone call to his or her mentor will trigger a chain of calls, notifying everyone in the group of that fact. As a cell group leader, I have often arrived at a hospital to discover several members of the person's cell group already present. The most powerful witness we can bring to observing unbelievers is our love *(agape)* and concern for one another. Centuries ago, an unbeliever named Pliny looked at the Christians of his day and said, *"See how they love one another, and there is nothing they will not do for each other!"*

But encourage one another daily, as it is called Today, so that none of you may be hardened by sin's deceitfulness.

Week 11, Day 5
This Week: The Journey Beyond
Today: Whitened Fields

Read Matthew 28:18-20; Acts 1:8; Romans 15:19-23

Thoughtfully read all the Scripture passages above. Then think for a while about these statements:

1. Jesus has assigned to *every child of God* the task of making disciples. That certainly includes you! Our major assignment is to bring others into the Kingdom. The word for "nations" in the Bible refers to *ethnic groups*, not geographical areas. Thus, it can refer to the Cantonese, the Kheks, the Huis, the Sundanese, the Uzbeks, the Mongols, etc. Satan knows that when all nations (ethnic groups) have heard the gospel, the end will come. For that reason, he seeks to trap human beings inside the prison walls of their cultures. Today, there are areas of the world with *no witness of Christ*. We are called to take the gospel to these people groups.

In Acts 1:8, Jesus told the disciples to begin discipling where they were, in *Jerusalem*. They were then to go to all the people in *Judea*. This area was the district surrounding the city of Jerusalem.

Next, they were to go to *Samaria*, an adjacent country, where people who were despised by the Jews lived. Finally, they were to go to *"the uttermost part of the earth."* This was not just an assignment for a few of His disciples, but to *all* who were with Him at the time.

> **Since this mandate includes you and me, write in your ethnic group equivalents to be found in the places mentioned:**
>
> **Jerusalem (your city):** _____
>
> **Judea (your area):** _____
>
> **Samaria (a nation nearby):** _____
>
> **The uttermost part of the earth . . .**
> **(Which country is halfway around the world**
> **from you?)**_____

Do you realize the Lord might assign you to go to another place to share His love with unreached people? He may do so! It may be within walking distance, or far away. *Are you willing to go?* For example, Houston, Texas has 92 different ethnic groups. Many of them live there without a single contact with Christians.

One cell group in Singapore looked at a huge population living in high-rise housing within walking distance of the area where they all lived. They began to visit in that area and soon had a new cell established in their *"Judea."*

Another cell group began to travel to an area where there were no known Christians an hour's walk away. They called it their *"Samaria."* They visited on weekends, met people, formed an evangelistic cell, and soon saw people following

Jesus and a new group of cells established. They knew that a cell group church has no geographical boundaries; it is a *movement*.

Chong Chee Yuen and Ruby were members of Faith Community Baptist Church in Singapore. Chee Yuen served as Zone Pastor of the North Zone until there were more than a thousand people in the cell groups. He and Ruby then went to Hong Kong to plant a church. They had extended the ministry of their home church to *"the uttermost part."* Churches have been planted in many parts of the world by cell members who took the Gospel to remote places. *All were established by people like you!*

2. The task of reaching people for Christ is *never* finished. Paul had come to the end of a journey, and looked back with satisfaction at the churches he had planted. He wrote, "So from Jerusalem all the way around to Illyricum, I have fully proclaimed the Gospel of Christ." He had one more destination: The "uttermost part" of his world was Spain.

Paul was not a "special Christian" when he wrote, *"It has always been my ambition to preach the gospel where Christ was not known"* (Romans 15:20). This should be the passion in our hearts.

There are three ways those in a cell group church do this. The *first way* is to be involved, with other members of the cell, in winning the lost and multiplying on a regular basis. A *second way* is for individuals in the cell to hear God's call to minister in the community around them, and to begin to lead a group and develop other groups. A *third way* is for God to call some to become part of a cell group church-planting team, to be sent to the "uttermost part."

When this happens, we become faithful stewards of what God has entrusted to us. We must all become *oikonomos* servants of the Lord, providing *"proper rations at the proper time"* for those God sends to extend the witness of the cell group church. As one cell group member said, "I have learned to live simply, in order that others can simply *live*."

✎ **Take a few minutes to read once more the scriptures assigned for today. Then go to the "Listening Room" and hear the voice of your Lord as He talks to you about what He has for you to do. Write your thoughts below:**

_____

_____

_____

_____

HOW TO SERVE AS A MENTOR

You have already completed *The Arrival Kit*, perhaps very recently. As you guide another person through the weekly discussions, you will also immensely profit from this experience! Not only will the review of the Scripture verses and the materials be worthwhile, but the relationship you develop with your protégé will also be unforgettable.

As you know, the purpose of *The Arrival Kit* journey is to help us re-evaluate our old values and add new Kingdom values. You are as important to this process as are the written materials! People's values change for many reasons. Sometimes the reason for the change is spiritual, but it can also be social or emotional. For example, I recently worked with a man who accepted Christ because he wanted to marry a Christian girl. As I worked with him, I had to be careful that he was not deceived by his motives. Becoming a Christian to please his fiancée might indicate that he has not made a true decision.

As you work with your protégé, be careful to ascertain why values are being changed or added. Saying *"I want to be a Christian"* may only be saying, *"I want to be different."* It doesn't always mean the person is totally surrendering all of his or her life to Jesus as Lord and Master.

People change most when they have a *model* to imitate. You will be a model as you serve as a mentor. Don't let that comment frighten you! You probably don't feel you are a model of a "perfect" Christian. *No one else is, either*. You will be adequate for the task as you make yourself available to Christ. Prayerfully accept your role as a model.

Above all, don't try to *fake* a level of spiritual life you haven't experienced. Sometimes the Holy Spirit uses your transparently honest life to do His work in another person's life.

Your protégé's journey into the Kingdom of God will not be entirely identical to yours. Comparing what has happened to you with what is taking place in someone else's life is not a good idea. *Scripture* is the measuring rod for Christian growth. Always use it as your yardstick.

WHAT CONSTITUTES SPIRITUAL GROWTH?

There are three reasons why you need to know what constitutes spiritual growth:

1. If you don't know what it is, you won't plan and work toward it.
2. If you don't know what it is, you'll accept any change as genuine. It's like shooting a bullet into a wall and then drawing a target around it to show you hit the bull's-eye.
3. If you don't know what it is, you may not see it when it takes place.

UNDERSTAND HOW PEOPLE GROW AS CHRISTIANS

People become Christians when they surrender their *minds* and *hearts* and *daily activities* to Christ's guidance. There is, of course, a moment in time when a person makes a decision to follow the Lord — but the actual *process* of salvation is the journey which follows. That's why Paul uses the continuous verb tense in Romans 10:10: We are to *"confess* and *confess* and *confess"* that Jesus is Lord. When we repent and journey toward making Jesus Lord of all, we become mature Christians.

The most important thing you can do for your protégé is to make this fact clear. As on-lookers, we are unlikely to know the exact moment a person becomes a true follower of Jesus Christ. All we can do is watch for signs that it is happening. Do not presume that a person is a growing Christian until you see evidence of it.

ASSUMPTIONS ABOUT YOUR PROTÉGÉ

1. *This person has prayed to receive Christ as Savior and Lord.*
2. *This person is literate.* A different approach to this version of *The Arrival Kit* may be needed for persons who do not learn by reading. Some are best helped by discussing the

truths mentioned in this book or by listening to cassette tapes. If you find your protégé learns in those ways, try sharing the contents of this book in a conversational way.

3. *This person is able to find Bible references.* As a mentor, you need to help a new believer who does not know how to find Scripture references. Refer the protégé to the listing of books in the "Table of Contents" page of the Bible.

HOW FAITH DEVELOPS: THE "MOVING TOWARD" STAGE

In Luke 3:8, John the Baptist said, *"Produce fruit in keeping with repentance."* The believer must prepare to live in the Kingdom of God by demonstrating sorrow for sins and turning away from them (repentance). This is called the *"moving toward"* stage of the Christian life. A praise song describes this stage with the words, *"Oh! I want to know you more!"* Does your protégé have that heart cry?

Before faith in Christ can become strong, there must be a *burning desire* in a person for his or her present condition to be changed. This often takes place through crisis events which interrupt the normal routines of life. For example, a seminary professor of mine was very cynical about "emotionalism" in other Christians until his own wife was stricken with meningitis and hovered at the point of death. As he cried out to God in his anguish, he confessed his intellectualism that had blocked his belief that God could heal. He prayed for her healing. As he *"moved toward"* the Father, he experienced a most profound sense of His presence.

Within a matter of hours, his wife's condition improved radically! He then realized that for years his lack of faith had hindered the power of God flowing through him as he trained pastors. He was never the same again in his teaching ministry.

Have you experienced this for yourself? Have there been moments when your heart cried out to God, *"Lord, more of You, and less of my selfish plans"*? If so, you know from your personal experience that there are very special times when we *"move toward"* the Lord. As you begin to work with your protégé, seek to discover if he or she has also had these "special moments" with the Holy Spirit. The first few times a person experiences this, a pattern is established. The strong emphasis on the "Listening Room" in the materials is designed to facilitate this.

Be aware that *The Arrival Kit* is not able to create that burning desire for change. For those who have it, this 11-week module can be very powerful. For others, it will simply be a task to be completed.

If your protégé is not *"moving toward"* God, you will sense lethargy and half-heartedness about spiritual things. If he or she does not have a thirst for God's best, what can you do about it? First, *pray and pray and pray* about the matter. You will be astonished to discover the changes that prayer will produce in your protégé. Second, *share your own longing for more of Christ's presence.* Burning desire is like any other fire — it sets aflame what comes into contact with it. Openly confess your deep desire to have more and more of God's presence ruling over you. In the presence of your protégé, cry out to God in prayer for a deeper presence of God in your life.

The aim of *The Arrival Kit* is to break the carnal values, strongholds, and practices of the believer. This includes earning money unfairly, materialism, sexual impurity, etc. It will be effective in the life of one who is in the *"moving toward"* stage. It will stimulate a desire for more time in the *"Listening Room"* and in faith-sharing with others.

HOW FAITH DEVELOPS: THE "MOVING TOWARD" STAGE

1. Do not give the impression that completing *The Arrival Kit* means he or she has "arrived." They have only taken a short journey into Kingdom living — that's all! There is much more to come.

2. Emphasize that being committed to the *daily* meditations in *The Arrival Kit* is very necessary. However, working through the materials in this book is not the same as making a deeper commitment to Jesus Christ.
3. Keep your objectives clearly in mind. Your protégé should:
   (1) Recognize the need to know God more;
   (2) Change lifestyles and values to fit Kingdom living;
   (3) Learn to *listen to God*.
4. Do not lay a guilt trip on your protégé if he/she comes and goes from the *"moving toward"* stage several times without making any strong commitment to Christ. In my experience in working with people, I have also encountered such vacillation in the spiritually immature. See it as a positive experience, not "backsliding." *Example:* Sam Lai was a Hong Kong drug addict and criminal, who came to Christ through a relationship with Dr. Jackie Pullinger. For months afterwards, Sam Lai went back and forth between his two worlds. Every time he returned, Jackie lovingly received him without rejection. I asked him, "Sam, how many times did you return to the old life and then come back to see Jackie?" He replied, "Ralph, it happened *scores of times*." Jackie was always there for him, encouraging him to take the next step. *Today, Sam is a church leader!*

There is no set length of time that a person remains in this *"moving toward"* stage. When a genuine commitment to seeking God and rejection of old values occurs, the next stage will be entered.

Before we think about the following stage, ask yourself:
(*Circle* Y = *Yes*; S = *Sometimes*; N = *No*)

Y   S   N   Do I long to know God more?

Y   S   N   Do my *own* values fit Kingdom living?

Y   S   N   Am *I* learning to *listen to God*?

HOW FAITH DEVELOPS: THE "LIVING IN" STAGE

The evidence of growth into godliness is in the honoring of God in different areas of life. This is the *"living in"* stage.

Faith is not *believing* something. It is the *activity* which takes place as a result of that belief. Growing in faith means I am putting each area of my life more completely in God's hands. It means I am releasing something to the control of Christ and accepting the outcome for it.

In this stage, there must be a direct power confrontation between old allegiances and the protégé's new allegiance to Christ. As a mentor, you will be in the best position to know what that will involve. It will nearly always involve being set free from inner strongholds. As you work through Weeks Seven and Eight, be sensitive to the need for deliverance in these sessions. Get help when necessary, either from your cell leader/shepherd, or someone recommended by him/her.

YOUR TASK: CREATE OWNERSHIP OF KINGDOM VALUES

Your protégé has already absorbed the *contents* of the material as the daily growth material has been studied. Do not teach it all over again when you meet! Your task is to help *apply* the truths to life situations.

Therefore, you will be provided with questions for each session. Use them to guide you in your times with your protégé. Note that the questions do not give you the privilege of lecturing! Rather, they will help you turn your knowledge into new ways of living. When we learn something *and then act upon it*, it becomes part of our value system. These are the questions you will ask in your weekly sessions:

1. What did you like best about this week's materials?
2. What did you like least about this week's materials?
3. What did you not understand?
4. What did you learn about God that you didn't know?
5. What do you personally need to do about it?
6. Which of this week's scripture memory verses is most significant for your journey?

Your effectiveness as a mentor will not be in how well you yourself have digested *The Arrival Kit* materials and re-teach them, but in how deep a relationship you build with the protégé. As you share your victories and struggles in your own journey, you will discover areas of mutual strengths and weaknesses. These will be used by the Holy Spirit to bring you closer to Christ and to each other. Sharing deeply is possible when you have moved from the "friendly" stage to the "deep trust" level. This may take three to four weeks to develop.

First Session: Getting Acquainted
Welcome to the Kingdom! (Pages 4-9)

You will meet once a week for 11 weeks with your protégé. Schedule a regular place and time to meet. When *The Arrival Kit* has been received, the protégé should complete pages 4-9 and then meet with you. *This initial session should bond your hearts together.*
1. Begin with the Quaker Questions
   Share with each other the responses to these four questions:
   • Where did you live between the ages of 7-12? How many brothers and sisters did you have?
   • What form of transportation did your family use?
   • Whom did you feel closest to during those years?
   • When did "God" become more than a word to you?

2. Compare your responses to the quizzes on pages 5 and 6.
   Bring your copy of *The Arrival Kit* with you to all the sessions, and openly share your written responses. Compare them with those of your protégé. Determine the similarities and differences in your answers.

3. Use the following topics when appropriate:
   • Share how you feel about being a mentor.
   • Explain how you have profited from the study of *The Arrival Kit*.
   • Share concerns that can become targets for mutual prayer.

Emphasize the importance of memorizing the Scripture verses. You might even help your protégé cut them out of the center pages.

Week 1
This Unit: Kingdom Lifestyles
This Week: Your New Family

It is essential that your protégé actually writes the answers to the quizzes in *The Arrival Kit*. Look over pages 10-19. This week, there are 12 quizzes to be completed using a pen or pencil. Look at your own answers, written weeks ago. Would you answer the same way today?

When you meet, look at all the pages for Week 1 in the protégé's book. Are *all* the quizzes filled in? If not, assist in completing all of them at the start of your session. Explain that we retain almost six times as much by *actually writing in* the answers than by only mentally responding. To ensure that your protégé remembers this, stress it is worth the effort to complete each quiz *using a pen or pencil*. If the questions have not yet been completed in writing, help the protégé to fill in the answers. Explain you will help each week to answer any questions that are not understood. *This is very important!*

Discuss the following questions:

1. What did you like best about this week's materials?
The major theme of this week is an introduction to the fact that Christians in the cell group are at different levels. There is a need for us to help one another. Was this clearly understood? You might include a discussion of the potential problems and conflicts he/she will see in the cell group, and the need for open communication among the members. Each meeting should be a time to build up one another.

2. What did you like least about this week's materials?
While this may seem like a very negative question to ask, it is an important way of surfacing personal problems or needs. For example, if your protégé is very hesitant about openly sharing with others, this week's material may reveal it. Ministry time may follow this question.

3. What did you not understand?
Areas that might be discussed include the difference between "Fathers," "Young Men," and "Little Children." Review the three levels of maturity. Perhaps mention can be made of persons in the cell group who are at these different stages.

4. What did you learn about God that you didn't know?
Knowledge of the nature of God should be progressive. Repeat this question each week, seeking to surface new insights into His character that have been revealed by the daily sessions. If the protégé does not have a clear reply to this question, spend some time reviewing what he or she does know about God and what may be confusing about His nature.

5. What do you personally need to do about it?
Every session should contrast present values with Kingdom principles. This is another time when special needs are shared. Take them seriously; delve into the history of these areas. Is there a need for release from bitterness, old habits, old fears? Minister as the Lord provides you with insights into the problems.

6. Which of this week's scripture memory verses is most significant for your journey?

The Scripture memory verses in *The Arrival Kit* were prepared with the assumption that Scripture memory verses have been given to your protégé at the time of his or her conversion. All new believers should learn the memory verses. They are:

1 John 1:9; 5:11-12; Proverbs 3:5-6; John 16:24;
1 Corinthians 10:13; and 2 Corinthians 10:3-4.

If those verses were not learned, you are encouraged to add them, one a week, as an extra Scripture verse to be memorized. Actually, memorizing three verses a week is not difficult if bits of time are constantly used for this purpose. *Examples: waiting for a bus, driving in a car, eating lunch alone, etc.*

Two verses have been selected for this week. Ephesians 2:19 seals the truth that we are "members of God's household." It emphasizes that the New Testament word for "household" actually refers to the cell group. Point this out, explaining that in the Scriptures the cell group is the first level of "God's household."

The second verse, 1 John 2:13, will seal in the protégé's memory the three levels of believers. As you discuss it, point out that every cell group will have people in these categories. One is not considered a "young man" spiritually until *after* he or she has *"overcome the evil one,"* and one is not considered a *"father"* until he or she has brought an unbeliever to experience the New Birth described by Jesus in John 3.

Week 2
This Unit: Kingdom Lifestyles
This Week: Let's Take a Tour

If your protégé is confused about how the domain of heaven, earth and the battleground mentioned in this week's materials, be prepared to review Ephesians 2:6 and Colossians 3:1, which explain that *spiritually* we are now *"seated with him in the heavenly realms."* These verses indicate we are now with Christ in heaven. Using Galatians 2:20, show that at the same time Christ is *in us* on earth, where we now live physically.

Thus, the Christian life is a supernatural life. We are with Him, and He is in us. The power of heaven is brought to earth by us as we *"bind and loose"* on earth that which has been *"bound and loosed"* in heaven (see Matthew 16:19). This is an amazing truth to be digested. We believers are actually the channels for the power of God to come from above to the earth!

1. What did you like best about this week's materials?

In each week's materials, one significant thought will impress the protégé. Spend special time developing all the ways it applies to the daily activities of life. It is expected that in some of the weeks you meet, the discussion of this first question may occupy most of your time together.

Do not be a slave to this outline. Be open to the direction of the Holy Spirit as you share together, and adjust the discussion accordingly.

2. What did you like least about this week's materials?

Ask specifically about the suggestion on page 23 that we can pray for one hour a day. From your own experience with *The Arrival Kit* materials, you know that in a later section a lot of stress has been given to the importance of the "Listening Room." This suggestion in Week 2 will be followed up in later weeks. If there is a negative response to the recommendation that one hour be spent in prayer, do not push it. People who are not moving toward God do not pray that long.

3. What did you not understand?
Significant truths about the condition of the earth today are presented in this week's materials. The fact that even the mountains and the seas "groan" because of the curse that has been caused by man's sin is an important truth.

4. What did you learn about God that you didn't know?
Somewhere in these 11 weeks, seek to get a full description of the way the protégé views the nature and character of God. Too often, believers avoid Him because their concept of Him is distorted. Is God seen as a "Grand Old Man" who overlooks our rebellion, or is He viewed as an angry "Man with a club," ready to smash us the moment we disobey? Believers who do not enjoy God will always avoid being with Him.

If it seems appropriate, mention some of these thoughts and probe the way God is perceived.

5. What do you personally need to do about it?
The "baggage list" in Day Five may be too personal for the protégé to share with you. Probe gently by asking, "What did the quiz on page 29 mean to you?" This may be a moment when *you* can transparently share *your* written responses. It is important that you ask, "Which baggage would you say gives you the most trouble *right now*?"

6. Which of this week's scripture memory verses is most significant for your journey?
The passage from Romans 8:38-39 is a great comfort in times of crisis! By memorizing it, the truth is readily available in moments when tragedy descends like a cyclone. Meditate together on how this verse relates to heaven, the battleground and earth.

The second passage, from Luke 17:20-21, stresses the place of the Kingdom of God in our world. *It is within us!* What does that mean? By the end of this session, the protégé should have a clear understanding of Kingdom life. Everywhere we go, everything we say, every act we perform connects the Kingdom of God within us to the world around us. *That's an awesome thought!*

Jesus allowed those He was training to do and say a lot of foolish things. In fact, those closest to Him seemed to make the biggest blunders. (Think of doubting Thomas and boisterous Peter!) If your protégé is genuinely trying to learn, you can put up with nearly any mistakes made. Keep seeing the best in your protégé!

Week 3
This Unit: The Kingdoms of This World
This Week: What's Old?

Working with your protégé should bring about a *"moving toward"* God. There are three parts to the process: the messenger (that's you), the message *(The Arrival Kit)*, and the receiver (the protégé). Which of these three parts should you focus on? Just as God adapted the way He communicated with men so also should our focus be on the *receiver*. He came to live among us so we would understand what He wanted us to know. You must imitate His methods by not focusing on yourself and your own needs. Think about the previous two sessions you have had together: Have you been totally concerned about what is relevant to the protégé? Think about these matters as you reflect on the following suggestions . . .

Was the exercise on page 33 completed?

This is the highest priority for your time together in Week 3. Turn *directly* to it and move on to the rest of the material as time permits.

It takes thought and concentration to complete *"My Value System, Part 1."* If the protégé avoided doing it, *do it together at this time.* This will be an excellent way for you to share more deeply about your own selection of values. Rating the values from 1 to 18 leaves lots of latitude for selecting the higher priorities. Ask, "What does it mean to put this value (ahead of, behind) the one you rated (above, below) it?"

We created this list of values by surveying people with different value systems. One interesting thing about the study was the rating given to "Doing the will of God." Among the unchurched, it was either last or next to last in all cases. Among the churched, it was rated somewhere among the first six — but was seldom selected as the very first value! Matthew 6:33 would be an excellent verse to tie in with this discussion.

Next, turn to Solomon's value system (page 35). Note that there are only two choices requested: the one Solomon might have ranked "1" and the one he might have ranked "18." Ask, "Do you think Solomon used the wisdom God gave him *wisely*? Why, or why not?"

1. What did you like best about this week's materials?
Or . . .
2. What did you like least about this week's materials?

Either what was liked *best* or *least* in the materials might well include the statement on page 30: "When you swear allegiance to the Kingdom of God, you must set aside your loyalty to a culture created by Satan." Discuss the elements of your culture that are demonic and those that are neutral. Is it possible to accept the values of the society you live in without contradicting the values of the Kingdom of God? What are areas of conflict for the protégé?

3. What did you not understand?

Is it plain to the protégé that there are fallen angels serving as controlling "princes" over every kingdom of this world? Perhaps a study of Daniel 10:20-21 would be appropriate. Living in the Kingdom of God requires us to know that we do not live in a universe where science can explain everything. The supernatural is beyond scientific examination.

4. What did you learn about God that you didn't know?

Discussing the topics studied this week will help you understand better your protégé's concept of God. As you ask this question week by week, you will grasp his or her understanding of the Father, the Son, and the Holy Spirit. He is the focus of our lives! The more we know Him, the more intimate will be our fellowship with Him.

5. What do you personally need to do about it?

Are you familiar with the day-to-day lifestyle of your protégé? Or, have you expected him or her to meet you on *your* turf and use *your* language? The responses to this question will have much more meaning if you personally meet the *oikos* people in his or her life.

6. Which of this week's scripture memory verses is most significant for your journey?

Galatians 3:26-28 places emphasis on our unity in Christ. Being "baptized into Christ" refers to the work of the Holy Spirit, which is then confirmed by water baptism.

Philippians 3:20-21 is a wonderful assurance that the Kingdom that is now within us will be consummated by the second coming of our Lord Jesus Christ.

Week 4
This Unit: The Kingdoms of This World
This Week: What's New?

In this week's materials, we are introduced to more than the Greek word *"oikos."* We are being presented with a concept that is key to understanding the church and how people come to Christ. Being sensitized to the *oikos* principle is one of the most important purposes of the studies in *The Arrival Kit*.

Prepare in advance the list of everyone in your *oikos* — your family, your business or school contacts, etc. Make sure that you include only those people you *consistently* talk directly to for a total of 60 minutes or more every seven days.

Share this list, indicating the spiritual condition of each person (unbeliever, believer, child, etc.). Then, make a similar list of those in your protégé's *oikos*. Discuss the spiritual condition of each person. Next, review the words *"oikonomos"* (pronounced "oi-kaw-naw-maws") and *"oikodomeo"* (pronounced "oi-kaw-daw-mé-oh"). Grasping these concepts should be a major goal of your time together in this session.

1. What did you like best about this week's materials?

In the discussion on this question, call attention to the illustration on page 49. Think together about the danger of Christians moving around each other constantly without ever "touching hearts" and ministering to one another. We must always remember that cell Groups are not, as a rule, model communities of good behavior. Rather, they are places where human *misbehavior* is brought out in the open, faced, and dealt with. As a hospital collects the sick, so also do cell Groups collect sinners. Traditional churches often leave these people undiagnosed. In a cell group, there is no way to disguise our problems. Ministering to one another is the very heartbeat of the cell group.

2. What did you like least about this week's materials?

Remember as you listen to the response to this question that it will give you special awareness of the concerns, fears, and perspectives of the protégé. The purpose of the question is to assist you to see more clearly how you can minister in these areas. Do not just gloss over or argue about what is said. Instead, prayerfully seek a word from the Lord about the way you can *oikodomeo* in the situation, "building up" your protégé with your sympathetic and objective response.

3. What did you not understand?

This question deals with the grasp of *information*, not *attitudes*. If there are any questions in the materials that you yourself do not understand, decide together whom you will consult for help — perhaps your own mentor, or your cell leader, or the cell leader intern. There is a lot of value in your joint search for answers to the questions in the materials. It is another way of bonding your hearts to each other. You will also discover, as you seek to explain what is not understood, that *you* will also grow in the process!

4. What did you learn about God that you didn't know?

The illustration on page 46 may help to stimulate sharing on this question if no strong response is forthcoming. The powerful truth of God being the *Source* of our resources has far-reaching implications. It means that for those in the Kingdom of God, there is no such thing as "luck." Buying lottery tickets, for example, is one way of saying, "I don't trust God to provide for me. I would rather let *chance* meet my needs." It also means that if God is seen as our Provider, we need never fear that we will not be properly cared for. A large percentage of the human race is driven by the fear of being penniless. The true believer rejects this fear! *God is our Provider.*

5. What do you personally need to do about it?

As this question is discussed once again, you have an open door to minister to your protégé. As the Lord guides you, probe the response and affirm commitments made to adjust values to align them with living in Christ.

6. Which of this week's scripture memory verses is most significant for your journey?

1 John 4:13 and 17 teaches us that our salvation is assured by the fact that *"he has given us of his Spirit."* Even as a pregnant woman never doubts that she has a child within her womb, so also the believer's assurance comes from the *inner presence* of the Holy Spirit. Ephesians 2:21-22 portrays the cell group as a building, constructed by Jesus Christ through the Holy Spirit.

Week 5
This Unit: The Servant Life
This Week: Equipped for Service

This week's material deals with two of the most important truths in Kingdom life: being completely filled with the Spirit and flowing in the spiritual gifts. The general introduction of *oikonomos* and *oikodomeo* in last week's materials was to prepare for these two important themes.

As you prepare your heart for this session with your protégé, think about the ways the Holy Spirit has made these two themes real for you. Of course, none of us feel that we have "arrived" at the fullness of His work in our lives. Where are *you* on the journey? During this sharing time, be prepared to talk and pray openly about your own walk. Remember the comments made on pages 124-126 about *"moving toward,"* etc. It would be good to read those pages again. Your ministry this week should be to help your protégé receive more of the presence and power of the Holy Spirit.

1. What did you like best about this week's materials?

Perhaps the response will refer to the teaching on "Come, Ask, Receive." This is an important truth to be *understood* as well as *applied.* What testimony from your own pilgrimage are you prepared to share? After these weeks together, a "deep trust" level should have developed between the two of you. Whatever your protégé "likes best" is an indicator of areas the Spirit has been dealing with. Take time to confirm these impressions.

2. What did you like least about this week's materials?

Once again, you are reminded that this question is not asked so you can gripe about the way the materials have been written, or voice your agreement or disagreement with what has been said. Your objective is to discern spiritual needs. Almost always, what has been "liked least" will be the area where the Holy Spirit is using sandpaper to expose some old values or attitudes.

3. What did you not understand?

The teaching about the gifts of the Spirit in this section may lead to many questions about the entire matter. Remember that the key chapters in your Bible about the gifts of the Spirit are found in Romans 12 and 1 Corinthians 12-14. Seek advice together, perhaps from one of the "fathers" in your cell group, on concepts of spiritual gifts you both do not understand.

4. What did you learn about God that you didn't know?

Was it important for your protégé to discover that the Holy Spirit can be *resisted, grieved, quenched,* or be the *Source of our being filled?* Often we think of the Holy Spirit as an object rather than as a Person. God's Spirit is not just a power that comes over us. He is a Person Who wishes to be in fellowship with us.

5. What do you personally need to do about it?

Each week, this question should lead you to minister through the spiritual dynamics taking place in the life of your protégé. Sometimes the sharing can be very intense. If it is, do not be in a hurry to move to the discussion of the Scripture memory verses. If your protégé desires to be filled with the Holy Spirit, pray with him or her for this experience.

6. Which of this week's scripture memory verses is most significant for your journey?

This week's verses are taken from Galatians. The first verse stresses the victory that is ours as we live and walk in the Spirit, and the conflict we can expect when both the sinful nature and the Holy Spirit co-exist within us. There is a major, unchangeable breakthrough in the Christian's life when the decision is finally made to *deliberately* walk in the Spirit!

The second verse is one of the classic statements of Paul and should be memorized by every believer. Notice that this verse does not refer to the *fruits* of the Spirit but the *fruit* of the Spirit. That is, we will not bear a *few* of these characteristics, but *all* of them simultaneously. In connection with it, you might like to tie it in with the previously memorized verse in Philippians 3:20-21 (week 3), which explains this future event takes place because Christ's power is now operating in us.

Be sure that you spend time reviewing previous verses memorized. If you are constantly reviewing them, they will not be forgotten. One must hear something six times before it is remembered. For long-term recall, the memorization review should be at least *ten times* that number. In other words, if verses are reviewed for *sixty days*, they will probably remain in your memory bank for a very long time.

Week 6
This Unit: The Servant Life
This Week: Touching God

The material this week may be the highlight of *The Arrival Kit* series for your protégé. You have carefully laid the foundation to present the truths relating to the "Listening Room." Most new (and many older) believers do not understand that prayer is actually a communion in which God speaks to us as much as we speak to Him! When we break through the barrier of one-way praying, our experiences with the Lord become electric, charged with His presence and power.

There are good reasons church historians have documented the lives of men who moved powerfully for God because of their prayer life. We must not let this Kingdom activity become second-rate. Before your meeting, it is a good idea for you to reflect on these pages, particularly reviewing the illustration on page 61.

1. What did you like best about this week's materials?
Your protégé may mention the material in Day 1, which indicates that God is *in us* when we pray to Him, and not in some remote spot of the universe. It's easy to avoid the *"God most high,"* but never the *"God most nigh!"* If another area of the material is mentioned in response to your asking this question, share fully about it. Then, return to mention this truth. Praying to the Christ Who dwells within us calls for transparency and confession of the highest level.

2. What did you like least about this week's materials?
By this time, the responses to this question may be revealing a pattern of the needs and struggles within the heart of your protégé. If so, take what you are sensing to the "Listening Room" and ask for guidance.

3. What did you not understand?
Understanding the whole issue of hearing God cannot be grasped by reading or talking about it. Nothing is more important to the Christian life than *experiencing it*. Remember that every believer *has already* had the experience of hearing God. The very act of accepting Christ is a response to His voice, calling us to repent and surrender ourselves to Him. Keep this in mind if this is mentioned when you ask this question.

4. What did you learn about God that you didn't know?
Was it the fact that He is *always speaking*? That's a great truth! He is never silent. Only our deaf ears cause Him to seem remote.

5. What do you personally need to do about it?
Give illustrations from your life about times when the Lord has spoken to you. For example, Crispen is a new believer who has grown in the Lord to the point that he is leading a cell group. Recently in his prayer life, the Lord gave him a word for a Christian lady who is married to an unsaved man. It was a word of assurance to her that her husband would indeed come to Christ. Since *"hearing God"* was a new experience for him, he pondered over telling her what the Lord had said. Finally, he did so — and discovered she had been praying for some assurance that he would come to Christ. Thus, *oikodomeo* took place and not *one*, but *two* lives were blessed because he had listened to God and had followed His leadership.

6. Which of this week's scripture memory verses is most significant for your journey?

Many people select Galatians 2:20 as their life verse (a verse chosen to be the key Scripture to be followed for life). Meditate on the powerful truths it contains. Every phrase has much for you to ponder upon! The assurance is given here that Christ is not far away, but is *within us*. You might discuss how this affects our prayer life. We must not picture Christ as far above the clouds when we pray; instead, our spirit communes with *His indwelling Spirit!*

The second verse, 1 Thessalonians 5:23, emphasizes the same theme from a slightly different perspective. We see God Himself active within every part of our being. Stress the meaning of the word "sanctify" used here. It means "set apart, made holy." You might mention that only God can *sanctify* us. We can *dedicate* ourselves to Him, but He is the only One Who can *consecrate* our lives. Note also this verse refers to "spirit, soul, and body." In connection with this, look together at the illustration on page 61.

Week 7
This Unit: Personal, Please
This Week: Dealing with Strongholds

1. What did you like best about this week's materials?

Minister to areas of strongholds mentioned by your protégé. Frankly discuss the importance of sexual purity. This area is often glossed over or never mentioned. Do not let this be bypassed in your sharing!

2. What did you like least about this week's materials?

Prayerfully respond to inner struggles over the contents of the materials.

3. What did you not understand?

Be sure the protégé recognizes that a *soul tie* is a relationship to a person, and that *idolatry* is a relationship to an *object*. Both soul ties and idols are areas of strongholds which may short-circuit the blessings of God in our lives.

Discuss the material on page 82 relating to the three stages of our salvation. There are many teachings floating around in the Christian world about "losing our salvation" if we commit particular sins. Scripture makes a strong distinction between being set free from the *penalty* of sin and being released from its *power*. Those who do not understand that truth often live in confusion, thinking that one slip into sin would undermine their salvation. No child can become a "non-child" by an act of disobedience! God is less willing to abandon His children than are human parents.

4. What did you learn about God that you didn't know?

Two key points from this week are (1) the awareness that God is always patient with us and (2) that He always despises sin in our lives.

5. What do you personally need to do about it?

Be sensitive to needs deeper than you can handle. Make referrals to your cell leader for persistent strongholds that need to be prayed over.

6. Which of this week's scripture memory verses is most significant for your journey?

Hopefully, the protégé has previously been given the first of the two Scripture verses, 1 Corinthians 10:13, prior to beginning *The Arrival Kit*. It is among the most basic Scriptures for memorization. Its value is in the assurance that whenever and wherever temptation comes, *there is a way of escape!* Hundreds and hundreds of believers will vouch for the power of this verse in their lives. Few people have their Bible handy when they face temptation. Therefore, hiding this verse in your heart provides protection in the most crucial moments.

The second verse, Luke 6:38, should lead you to discuss the use of wealth and the importance of investing in the Lord's work. Scripture makes it plain that a tithe of our earnings belongs to the Lord, and not to offer it to Him is spiritual thievery. Does your protégé tithe? If not, why? This matter should be discussed and settled once and for all at this time. Give your personal testimony of the joy tithing has brought to your own life.

Week 7 — Addendum
Special Facts About Strongholds
for You to Consider

When a farmer prepares soil for a new crop, he first removes all the rocks, roots, and stumps that would keep the soil from being fruitful. The strongholds (rocks, roots, and stumps) in the life of the believer must be removed. Mark 4 speaks of believers that are "good soil," able to receive the word of God as seed, producing fruit thirty, sixty, and a hundredfold.

If, for whatever reasons, your protégé is unwilling to come to Jesus, laying down *all* idols and soul ties, and confessing *all* known sins, a deliverance ministry is not yet possible. Continue to pray for this person to be set free. Jesus said our heart is where our treasure is — and if something or someone is treasured more than God, no release is possible at this time. Some people feel guilty about allowing sinful situations to remain, but their ties are so strong that they will not cut off that which is evil. They live under the condemnation of their sin and their personalities reveal this through depression, anger, or despair.

On the other hand, we are to experience *total* freedom in Christ! Satan is a legalist. He knows his rights and will take advantage of every permission we give him to occupy territory in our lives. When he is denied access, he must flee. Seek assistance in ministry to your protégé if the needs are greater than your experience can handle. I strongly recommended that you prayerfully sit in on any ministry time that takes place with your protégé. You alone will be in a position to continue the affirmation — and call to accountability — of deliverance and commitments made during such times.

Week 8
This Unit: Personal, Please
This Week: Dealing with Attitudes

Last week's materials are crucial to the life of the protégé. The discussion about strongholds was deliberately planned for the seventh week. A foundation has been laid. Another 4 weeks remain for you to work with him or her before this module is completed. Was there a desire for deliverance from strongholds, or a resistance to it? This question will strongly guide your ministry from this point on.

Many believers live in a stronghold of *negative attitudes*. They are among the greatest of all Satan's deceptions. Indeed, happiness comes from *choosing* to live out Kingdom values.

1. What did you like best about this week's materials?

What about the discussion of the weaker brother? Is that an area of dislike? Does your protégé feel a real responsibility for those who have been in the cell group? Walking in love toward the other members may be difficult to do. We often find negative feelings within ourselves toward people we do not enjoy being around. Will Rogers was far from being a strong follower of Christ, but he said these classic words: "I never met a man I didn't like!" Every Christian should be able to say that! The significance of others is not based on their performance!

2. What did you like least about this week's materials?

Day 5 is a further reference to a common stronghold in the lives of believers — bitterness in the heart. What was the response to this issue? Is a discussion about this matter now possible? You may want to share this prayer at this time:

Father, in the name of Jesus, I have not loved the following person (insert name) who has hurt me. I ask You to help me forgive, love, and understand (him, her) as only You can do. I ask this in the name of Jesus and for the sake of my life lived with Him leading my actions. Amen.

3. What did you not understand?

Deal openly and transparently with Day 2's discussion of the way we relate to other people. In a world filled with lust, no Kingdom value is more important than a right view of human bodies. In counseling young men, I have learned that a majority of them first discovered pornography by finding their father's secret collection. In many of these cases, the fathers were not only believers, but were office holders in a church. Lust is widespread. We must not gloss over an issue that is dealt with so squarely in Scripture. Frankly discuss this and any same-sex attraction your protégé might be struggling with or hiding.

4. What did you learn about God that you didn't know?

The total and complete forgiveness of God is something we often do not understand. We *expect* Him to forgive us, because He promised to do so — but then we live as though His forgiveness was not adequate enough to bring us happiness. Every time we do this, we are actually elevating ourselves above Him. We are saying, "God forgave me because He is God. *But I cannot forgive myself.*" To do this is to position our forgiveness of ourselves as higher than His forgiveness of us. This causes us to "play God" with our own lives. Thus, we rob Him of His rightful place as King of kings.

5. What do you personally need to do about it?

The only way a person can be freed from strongholds is to walk in repentance and in submission to the Lord. One-time prayers of surrender, which are not followed by a walk of faith, do little to change value systems. After these weeks together, you can evaluate whether earlier commitments are leading to a permanent change in behavior. If not, prayerfully review earlier commitments made, and challenge your protégé to be faithful to them as vows made to the Lord. Our cell group relationships are a powerful way to help one another!

6. Which of this week's scripture memory verses is most significant for your journey?

Romans 14:7-8 is a wonderful VERSE to carry through life, and into the valley of the shadow of death as well. The time to memorize it is long before eternity is faced! I will never forget a precious man in a church I pastored whose name was Eugene Rissmeyer. In his late forties, he was struck down with cancer. As I visited him week after week, he slipped into the final stages of suffering. One day, he said to me, "When you preach at my funeral, this is the text you are to use. It is my final witness." He then quoted this passage from Romans 14.

The second verse, 1 Corinthians 9:22-23, relates to our witness to the unreached people in our lives. It describes the spirit of servanthood, which must exist as we share our Lord with others. The final phrase, *"that I may share in its blessings"* describes the value system of Kingdom people. We never do anything for the Lord out of a sense of guilt. We do it because we know we will be blessed as a result.

Week 9
This Unit: Facing the Powers
This Week: The Battle for Men's Souls

Far too often, Christians settle into a passive, introspective form of Kingdom life. If Satan cannot neutralize the witness of believers by tempting them with *evil* deeds, he delights in doing so by making them perform *good* deeds that divert them from spiritual warfare. The final three weeks of *The Arrival Kit* focus on reaching out to unbelievers. Future equipping will focus on evangelism as the cell group and its members reach the lost. As you review the materials in Week 9, give attention to the material in Day 1. It is an introduction to the rest of this book.

1. What did you like best about this week's materials?

The material on *"praying until"* is provided to strengthen the desire of the protégé to spend quality time in the "Listening Room." If this topic is the one mentioned in response to this first question, affirm the value of such prayer activity. It would be most valuable for you to add your own testimony to those of the material: what has happened when you have *"prayed until"*? Standing in the gap (page 99) has brought many an unbeliever to Christ. You might discuss the names of your *oikos* friends who are not believers, and seek to apply this form of prayer life to them. Are these contacts *unprotected* from the power of the evil one because there is no prayer barrier being raised for them? Is it possible for the two of you to set apart some time to pray for them?

2. What did you like least about this week's materials?

In sharing the thoughts of this week, some have balked at accepting *personal responsibility* for the salvation of the lost. Of course, this is Satan's best weapon. If he can convince the soldiers not to enter the battleground, he has won without firing a shot.

3. What did you not understand?

Was the contrast between the motives of Father God and Satan understood? Is it recognized that *nothing* Satan offers is done out of a spirit of benevolence? If this course can create an awareness of the character of the enemy, the *"little child"* will become a *"young man"* who has *"overcome the evil one"* (see 1 John 2:13-14).

4. What did you learn about God that you didn't know?

Was it the realization that our significance in God's eyes has *nothing to do with our work for Him*? For most of us, it was overwhelming to discover that we are loved simply because we are His children. God never withholds His love because of wrongs we have done. We do not ever have to fear that He will abandon us when we have displeased Him.

5. What do you personally need to do about it?

Hopefully, one of the emphases you will discuss is your mutual desire to reach out to *oikos* people who need to receive the Lord as Master. A life of serving the Lord involves constant contact with those we know who do not know Him.

You might wish to meditate together on the words found on page 103: *"It is the task of a servant to obey his Master; it is the obligation of the Master to provide for that servant. Therefore, the servant need never be afraid!"*

6. Which of this week's scripture memory verses is most significant for your journey?

Both the Scriptures for this week stress a truth that must be internalized by you and your protégé: God's greatest desire is that *everyone* should come to repentance. We must grasp this as the primary motivation for everything that our Father does. Too often we think we are pleasing Him by the total time we spend in prayer, Bible study, or some form of Christian service. Satan most powerfully seeks "good things" as roadblocks to keep us from doing the "right thing." God wants *everyone* to come to repentance — *everyone!* For me and for you, that means *every single person we know!*

To have memorized these verses is to think about how God will totally revolutionize all that we do. Entrance into the Kingdom is to be offered to all men and women everywhere. That universal truth must be broken down into *oikos* parts. That's where each of us gets involved. Share together the impressions these two verses have made in your lives as you have committed them to memory.

By the way, have you been taking time to *review* the verses from previous weeks? Don't let them pass in and out of your memory bank. It is as important for *you* to share them aloud as it is for you to check your protégé's memorization.

Week 10
This Unit: Facing the Powers
This Week: The Wrestling Match

Have you been faithful in reviewing the written responses to the questions, which are to be completed as your protégé works through the materials? At least 60% of the impact of the material will be lost if this is not done. Each query is designed to help your protégé digest what has been read.

1. What did you like best about this week's materials?

This week focuses our attention on the battleground where those in the Kingdom of God must practice warfare. In the weeks ahead, you and your protégé should be witnessing together to unbelievers. You will quickly discover that at the exact moment a person is ready to accept Christ, Satan will interfere. Literally hundreds of times through my life, I have seen the evil one interrupt! A dog will bark. The baby will throw a tantrum. People will drop by unexpectedly. Just a few evenings ago, I was at the point of helping a 72-year-old man pray to receive Christ, and a total stranger pulled up in the drive and began to blow his horn incessantly. He finally discovered he was at the wrong house. *Was it a coincidence?* Not at all — it has happened too many times. Therefore, the materials this week seek to sensitize your protégé to some basic warfare principles. The principalities and powers don't bother a Christian who is not threatening their domain, but the moment we storm the "gates of hell", there will be a battle. Therefore, getting acquainted with the armor and weapons of our warfare is important. Note the comment at the end of page 105, explaining that "they should be worn as our everyday garments, not just put on at special times."

2. What did you like least about this week's materials?

If your protégé has a scientific worldview, the very thought of angels and demons and principalities may seem far out. This is true. These creatures *are* far out — they have no place at all in the Kingdom of God, but they certainly do exert their presence in the kingdoms of this world. If there are doubts in your protégé's mind about the reality of all that is taught this week, take a swift journey together through the first ten chapters of Mark. Review the many reports listed there of Jesus' encounter with the supernatural.

3. What did you not understand?

There are many books written that will help to expand your understanding of spiritual warfare. A 1992 release by Peter Wagner, *Warfare Prayer*, is recommended.

4. What did you learn about God that you didn't know?

In the materials for Day 3, it is explained that Christ Himself is the armor we wear. He is our protection as well as the Source of our power. The One Who sends us into battle is Himself our protection.

5. What do you personally need to do about it?

Learning about spiritual warfare from a book is like putting your big toe into the water to determine what the ocean is like. The response to this training must be *actual ministry to the unconverted*. Only in such encounters against Satan's domain will we learn what it costs to bring the lost to Jesus. Bringing the lost to Jesus is our ultimate goal! As I was writing this page, the telephone rang. A friend in India called to tell me about a horrible beating a pastor had received at the hands of officials. If the villagers had not interfered, the man would have been murdered. This is the work of Satan! *There are casualties in warfare.*

6. Which of this week's scripture memory verses is most significant for your journey?

This week's Scriptures both focus on spiritual warfare, which is a constant activity for Kingdom residents. We must never forget that we are part of the army of God, and that we have been given the spiritual resources to be victorious. In Ephesians 6:12, the enemy is described for us. This enemy is on the *"battleground,"* where the forces of evil come to destroy and devour. Our armor is presented in the second passage, found in Ephesians 6:17-18.

Take some time to meditate together on the truths in these passages. Can you recognize the presence of those *"rulers, authorities, powers of this dark world and spiritual forces of evil in the heavenly realms,"* you sense exist in your present circumstances? What is the significance of attaching the prayer life of Ephesians 6:18 with *"praying for all the saints"*? Meditate on the responsibility this phrase calls for — we are to be responsible for those in our cell group.

Week 11
This Week: The Journey Beyond

Plan to celebrate during this final meeting. Your protégé has worked hard to complete *The Arrival Kit*. Through this process you have probably noticed that he/she has matured as a believer of Jesus. Congratulate your protégé. Honor this person with a card, small gift, lunch, etc. Look for ways to make this person feel special! Before you meet together, review the material and questions, consider the way(s) you will celebrate, and consider how you will bring closure to this facet of your relationship.

1. What did you like best about this week's materials?

Did the concept of being God's priests make an impression? In what way did it make an impression? It is an honor to be a representative of the Lord God among the children of darkness. A priestly life is the greatest level of servanthood. It is worthwhile to review together page 116.

2. What did you like least of all in the materials?

Did you feel overwhelmed in thinking that you need to continue growing — being equipped for Kingdom service? Those who have taken their Kingdom journey seriously know that being equipped is the result of loving Christ. We never find joy in doing things out of obligation — only out of overflow. A believer who is content with mediocrity in his or her walk with the Lord is not in the phase of *"moving toward."* If, however, your protégé desires to be thoroughly equipped, you will take the next steps.

3. What did you not understand?

Do you remember the verse from 1 Peter that spoke of God choosing you? Even mature Christians will occasionally struggle with the idea that God chose them. But know that Peter was speaking of you when he wrote: *"you also, like living stones, are being built into a spiritual house to be a holy priesthood, offering spiritual sacrifices acceptable to God through Jesus Christ. . . . But you are a chosen people, a royal priesthood, a holy nation, a people belonging to God, that you may declare the praises of him who called you out of darkness into his wonderful light. Once you were not a people, but now you are the people of God; once you had not received mercy, but now you have received mercy"* (1 Peter 2:5, 9, 10).

4. What did you learn about God that you didn't know?

Was it the statement on page 122 that Jesus has assigned to every child of God the task of making disciples? Satan does his best to keep that fact from new believers. He rejoices when reaching the lost is delegated to a committee, or to the *"paid professionals"* of the church. The God Who is not willing that any should perish has a common assignment for us all. No one is excluded.

5. What do you personally need to do about it?

Maturing as a believer means that you will serve others. Does the idea of being a minister to someone else make you feel apprehensive about continuing the journey? What actions can you and will you take to ensure that you continue to grow? What actions will you take to ensure that you faithfully serve God and serve people?

6. Which of this week's scripture memory verses is most significant for your journey?

The last two Scriptures in *The Arrival Kit* summarize our position in Christ. We are *"in Him,"* and He is *"in us."* Our faithfulness or faithlessness does not change His response to us. His love is not a reward for our obedience. *"Reigning with Him"* is a future event, but it also takes place at this very moment. He indwells us; so His reign takes place wherever we go and whoever we influence. Since we are His property, *"he cannot disown Himself."*

Is there any better reason we can think of to follow the directive of 2 Timothy 2:15 to be a *"workman"* in the Kingdom? The term *"the word of truth"* is explained in Ephesians 1:13 and Colossians 1:5 as *"the gospel of your salvation."* Thus, while the term is used elsewhere to refer to the entire Bible as the *"word of truth,"* here it speaks of the Gospel that brings salvation. Thus, the task of the *"workman"* revolves around sharing the Gospel, not just becoming a sequestered, isolated student of Scripture.

VERIFICATION OF COMPLETION

As the cell leader for

_____

(Name of cell member:)

I have reviewed this copy of The Arrival Kit and I certify
that the work has been completed.

Signed:_____ Date:_____

CPSIA information can be obtained
at www.ICGtesting.com
Printed in the USA
LVOW13s1456090518
576563LV00022BA/653/P